50 SPORTS WARES

Innovations in Design and Materials

Mel Byars

Introduction by
Aaron Betsky

Research by
Cinzia Anguissola d'Altoé
Brice d'Antras
Matthias Brühlmann
Kara Johnson
Yanitza Tavarez

Technical drawings by
Marvin Fein

A RotoVision Book

PRO DESIGN SERIES

 RotoVision

RotoVision

Published by RotoVision SA
Rue du Bugnon, 7
CH-1299 Crans-Près-Céligny
Switzerland

RotoVision SA
Sales & Production Office
Sheridan House
112/116A Western Road
Hove, East Sussex, BN3 IDD, England
Tel: +44 (0)1273–7272–68
Fax: +44 (0)1273–7272–69
e-mail: Sales@RotoVision.com

Distributed to the trade in the United States
Watson-Guptill Publications
1515 Broadway
New York, NY 10036
U.S.A.

10 9 8 7 6 5 4 3 2 1

06 05 04 03 02 01 00 99

ISBN 2-88046-418-8

This book was written, designed, and
produced by Mel Byars.

Printed in Singapore
Production and separation
by ProVision Pte Ltd, Singapore
Tel: +65 334–7720
Fax: +65 334–7721

PRO DESIGN SERIES

50 Chairs: Innovations in Design and Materials
by Mel Byars with an Introduction by Alexander von Vegesack

50 Tables: Innovations in Design and Materials
by Mel Byars with an Introduction by Sylvain Dubuisson

50 Lights: Innovations in Design and Materials
by Mel Byars with an Introduction by Paola Antonelli

50 Products: Innovations in Design and Materials
by Mel Byars with an Introduction by David Revere McFadden

50 Sports Wares: Innovations in Design and Materials
by Mel Byars with an Introduction by Aaron Betsky

Contents

Introduction:
Game Over? Sports in the Age of Cyborgs

By Aaron Betsky
Curator of Architecture, Design and Digital Projects
San Francisco Museum of Modern Art

There is a natural relationship between experimental design and sports. Design that is not content to make us comfortable pushes itself to the edge, while in sports the whole point of the exercise is to push your body to that same ledge. Going all the way to the extremes of what the body can do and where it can go necessitates the right equipment. We need stuff that pushes the very boundaries of materials, forms, and even the definition of what an object is. As Mel Byars shows in this witty collection of masterful objects, the results are often things that have only vague resemblances to the bicycles, the helmets, the golf clubs, or even the green grass we might remember. Instead, many of these objects are reaching toward a symbiosis with the human body. In sports, we are becoming one with our gear. That is where design in general is leading in an age of ergonomics, "human factor" design, and wearable brand logos, but in sports it just does it.

The most obvious relationship between sports equipment and the body occurs when we seek to clad our bodies in ways that let us go to places where we were probably never intended to be. The Metaltex clothing (pp. 68–69) is the most obvious example of such a second skin. The Animal wet suit (pp. 72–74) takes the idea a step further by padding the body to the point where it begins to resemble something not quite human. In backpacks, such as the Auret 55 (pp. 66–67), a smooth and symmetrical extension of the body replaces the clunky box we used to carry with us. In all cases, the appearance of the body itself becomes smooth, abstract, and altered.

Not all objects mold themselves this clearly to the body. While the Halfdome Mountaineering helmet (pp. 90–93) is an abstract version of the skull itself, the X-O Skeleton Mountaineering helmet (pp. 94–95) is, if anything, a tracing of the folds of the brain itself mapped onto some theoretical mountain. The designers of some of the most advanced equipment intended to protect us from the elements have realized that our bodies might need to change shape in a fairly radical way in order to survive in alien surroundings. Science fiction becomes reality as we venture not to Mars but to the farthest reaches of the Himalayas, and our feet and arms begin to resemble the animals that survive in such hostile terrain.

There is a tendency among objects of motion to become almost like the body itself, as is evident in the humorously named Ina Zone kayak (pp. 44–45). The devices that keep us in motion must mediate between us and the nature around us. At their best, they therefore become something as minimal as possible, molding themselves as closely as possible to our muscles and limbs that are doing the work. In this way, as little energy as possible is lost in its transfer to objects of motion, which in turn shape themselves to the wind, the water, or the terrain in such a way that every bit of material not scoured down by these forces manipulates them to increase our speed.

The result is the design of objects that are slick, sleek, and altogether strange in appearance. Yet, just as not all cladding mimics the outside appearance of our bodies directly, there is also another way for an object to keep us going: by creating a rugged connection between us and the natural environment. This is the direction taken by mountain bicycles and so gloriously expressed by the Lobo Downhill (pp. 52–55). Here a vestige of the industrial revolution has become honed down to efficient perfection. The Lobo is a tool that turns with precision-engineered gears in a highly precise manner. It functions in this manner not so that we can extract natural resources from the earth (as was the purpose of most industrial equipment) but so that we can experience that same earth. Crampons (pp. 104–105), which allow us to cling to vertical ice walls, offer an aggressive contrast to such designs as the Cubic 3X Skating ski (pp. 78–79). With the crampons, it is almost as if our inner sinews that do all the real work stand revealed in metallic form.

Then there are those objects that have no direct relationship to preserving our bodies or propelling us. They are rather ones that extend our reach and our domain so that we can play. From the Copperhead bat (pp. 18–20) that boosts our swinging power with electricity to the Fun Rang boomerang (pp. 32–35) that lets an abstract mandala of joy arc through the air, these toys let us hit or throw things and otherwise engage our environment in more and more powerful ways. They are prosthetics, like eye glasses or artificial legs, that replace our body's meager possibilities with objects that have been paired down for one specific function.

It is perhaps no coincidence that these objects are now beginning to resemble the accouterments of kings or priests. The shamanistic overtones of our golf clubs and our tennis racquets and even the mystical symbols we paint on our skateboards connect these objects to a world that is resolutely not the everyday. Their strange shapes make the arcs of balls into something real. And the world of AstroTurf (pp. 148–150) is a special realm. Together, this equipment hints at a highly ritualized rhythm to which we surrender ourselves exactly to escape the boundaries of the mundane.

The irony of all of these design vectors of escape is that the machinery enslaves us ever more. Most of us engage in sports to get away from the routine of everyday life. We want to escape from the tasks we are forced to perform and from the imprisoning sites where we work. At the heart of the notion of sports is the stripping down of culture to the point that we can confront the world around us with nothing more or less than our bodies. Yet to do this, we must either enter the highly regularized world of competitive sports or pour ourselves as much as we possibly can into as much of the technology that drives that same culture. All this, of course, we do after we have been transported by planes, trains, automobiles, or, these days, even helicopters as far away as possible.

The most extreme version of this dilemma is the gym equipment into which we strap ourselves so that we can change our bodies. In some cases now, these torture racks are fitted with virtual-reality displays so that we can pretend we have escaped technology completely. This would seem

to offer the ultimate answer to the need of the modern sports enthusiast: the most complete and immediate challenge to the body in the most remote and fantastic setting. All this would also seem to be design at its most basic. We create either themed environments or efficient equipment that mimics the body. Except for the logos we apply to our objects, the objects themselves have become less and less recognizable as being separate from us. In sports, however, the extreme nature of the enterprise appears to guarantee that something will remain.

That which is not honed down to fantasy or function is exactly that which animates many of the designs collected here: gadgets that display the sheer love of invention. Sometimes, after all, the game is not about winning, losing, or playing but rather having the right equipment.

Foreword:
To Be Superhuman

By Mel Byars

There is no doubt that the design of sports equipment and clothing is fascinating. By their very nature, sports wares extend and enhance the puny possibilities of the naked human body. Sports equipment encourages performance which our own unaugmented frames and pitifully inadequate muscles are incapable of realizing. Helmets make our crania stronger; skis and boards enlarge our narrow feet; bicycles permit travel with abnormal speed; clothing creates transpiration to sustain our energy; chronometers inform us of our ability; photographic timers and computers tell us who won, placed, and showed.

More than ever, we have more leisure time and it seems we are more competitive. We have a need to have fun and to be better than others. And many of us have more money than our parents had. Sports industries are exploiting this new-found obsession and wealth, and the thrust is supporting the development of expensive new technologies, materials, and thus designs.

The pace of new developments in sports equipment has become very fast. Were the publication of this book to be postponed for a few years, it would be out-of-date. To illustrate this fact on the following pages, an inline skate of 1992 (pages 134–137) has been included as a foil to an inline skate of 1997 (pages 138–140). The dissimilar examples were designed by the same studio for the same firm. A visit to any sports museum will reveal the phenomenon of this obsolescence. And, for contemporary comparisons, there are contrasting skis, skates, skateboards, boots, and helmets here that were developed during more or less the same period of time by different designers for different manufacturers.

Like the other volumes in the Pro-Design Series, the quest for visual documentation and detailed information for *50 Sports Wares* challenged and provoked the researchers and me. We needed adequate visual documentation and detailed information in order to fulfill the imperative of the book. Unlike other books about design, a single pretty picture of a product was inadequate. We sought good photographs, drawings, a list of materials, an explanation of how they were exploited, and a clear description of the processes employed. With long lists, we approached

manufacturers and designers who frequently thwarted our mission. We experienced indifference, ignorance, procrastination, and indolence. In addition, some had not retained documentation or were unwilling to give it to us.

Fortunately, other manufacturers and designers were graciously forthcoming, and the results of their magnanimity have made this book possible. But none was paid by me or the publisher for inclusion here, and some of them are represented by more than one example of their work. The book is also indebted to the intelligence and fortitude of the researchers, Cinzia Anguissola d'Atoé of Milan, Brice d'Antras of Paris, Matthis Brüllmann of Basel, Kara Johnson of Cambridge, England, and Yanitza Tavarez of New York City. This book would simply not have been possible without them.

As someone who is unathletic and inexperienced in every sport, I may be both the worst and the best person to write this book. As the worst, I know nothing of the dynamics of a sport one can acquire only through experience. Therefore, I was beholden to designers' and manufacturers' explanations. Many of them are sportspeople adept at one or another sport, and, additionally, many collaborated with manufacturers' experts to develop equipment that would satisfy rigid performance standards and the demands of the marketplace. As the best or, more accurately, an adequate person who served as voyeur, I took nothing for granted in attempting to understand the essentials of the design solutions. I asked dumb questions to get the kind of answers that someone experienced in a sport might have incorrectly assumed to know.

The categories of Equipment, Vehicles, Bodywear, Boards—Skis, Vehicles, Head Gear, Footwear, and Etcetera give the book form, but the arbitrary organization may be faulty. For example, why are crampons footwear and not skis? Is a backpack bodywear? Why isn't a wrist timer—possibly soon embedded under the skin—bodywear?

The best contribution that this book may make is its glimpse into the wide world of contemporary sports wares—creations born of the minds and hearts of some of today's most imaginative and ardent designers and manufacturers.

Equipment

MaxGlo tennis ball

Designers: Dunlop staff
Manufacturer: Dunlop Racquet Sports Division, Greenville, SC, U.S.A.
Date of design: 1999

The game of tennis reaches back beyond 1308 when King Philip IV built a tennis court in the hôtel de Nesle, one of the earliest indoor courts in Paris. In 1351, tennis became an open-air game in England. Earlier tennis balls were, of course, handmade crude versions compared to today's, like this example which the manufacturer claims to be like no other and the best. It is composed of 14 ingredients in the rubber core alone, and the core is covered by a blend of cotton and the finest wool from New Zealand. Dunlop's fastidious concerns extend to the air-tight container that keeps the balls at a certain, ideal air pressure.

Pure, high-quality rubber from Malaysia is analyzed at the source to assure quality and consistency.

Fourteen special ingredients are compounded and blended for the final formula.

Blanks, or large pellets, are extruded in precise amounts and accurately weighed under controlled conditions.

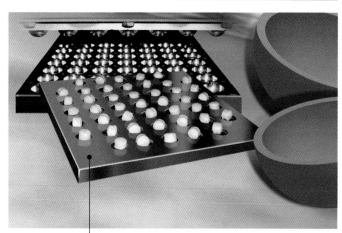

Blanks are placed in a precision automated half-shell mold and formed under controlled high pressure and temperature.

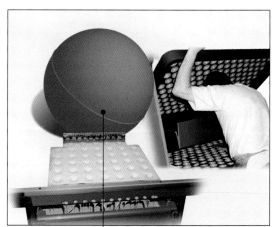

Shell edges are sanded, and a solution of natural rubber is applied to the edges. The half shells are then vulcanized or sealed together in a press under heat and pressure before being sanded. Thus, a hollow rubber ball is formed.

Continued on next page

MaxGlo tennis ball

To protect and preserve the ball's life and enhance performance, the hollow rubber ball is bonded to a highly durable cloth made of cotton and natural New Zealand wool that the manufacturer calls MaxGlo.

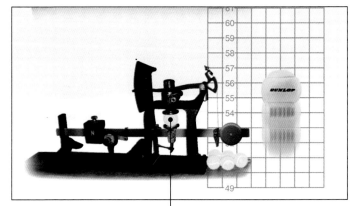

After a ball is steamed and dried, each is hand-inspected and monitored by a series of tests and inspections which simulate the impact and abrasion caused during normal play. Additionally, a ball is uniformly tested for accurate flight characteristics, aerodynamics, and bounce.

The cloth cover
is bonded to the
rubber core by
vulcanization.

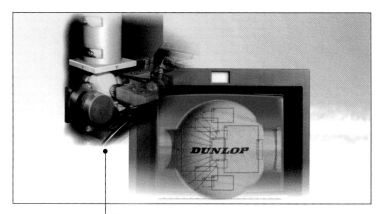

Further tests are performed
before the balls are packed in
hermetically sealed, pressurized
cans to keep the inner pressure
of the balls at 15 lbs/sq. in.

TiS5, TiS6, and TiS7 titanium tennis racquets

Project team: Johan Eliasch, president/C.E.O.; Robert Marte, division manager; Claus Müller, product manager; Herfried Lammer, research-&-development head, and Markus Hämmerle, communications manager
Manufacturer: Head Sport A.G., Kennelbach, Austria
Date of design: 1997

The manufacturer claims that its unique combination of titanium and graphite has produced the lightest, most powerful racquet ever made. With the introduction of the TiS7 in 1997, Head became the first manufacturer to produce a high-performance racquet in titanium. The TiS6 is the best-selling racquet worldwide, according to several respectable independent studies. Much of the success may be due to the efforts of engineer Herfried Lammer, who holds a degree in plastics-technology engineering. However, the ITF (International Tennis Federation) has deemed the TiS7 unacceptable due to the string surface's exceeding 15.5in.

	TiS5	TiS6	TiS7
Cross section:	27mm	29mm	29mm
Head size:	107sq. in.	115sq. in.	124sq. in.
	(690cm)	(742cm)	(800cm)
String weight:	9oz	8.9oz	8.7oz
	(255g)	(252g)	(247g)
Length:	extra long	extra long	extra long
Grip size:	1–5	1–5	1–5
Grip:	SofTac	SofTac	SofTac
String pattern:	16/19	16/19	16/20
Speed:	moderate-slow	medium	slow
Machinery for construction:			
	robots and spray painters		
Assembly:	carbon pre-pregs and titanium/graphite		
	pre-pregs		

Factory capacity: 4,500 racquets per day

Using computer technology, experience, and the competitiveness of athletes, Head's technical staff was able to create a racquet one-third lighter than those of only a few years ago.

Areas of the testing facilities.

The frame is tested. Extra-strong titanium is woven with ultra-light high-modulus graphite fibers to form a very stiff, very strong construction which thwarts twisting.

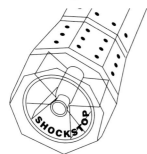

The ShockStop mechanism makes play more comfortable and eliminates the pinging sound normally produced by wide-bodied racquets. The device reduces racquet vibration 90% faster than conventional racquets, according to the manufacturer.

Copperhead ACX

Designers: Worth staff
Manufacturer: Worth, Inc., Tullahoma, TN, U.S.A.
Date of design: 1998

Worth became known in the 1940s for introducing the first raised-seam softball. It allows for better grip control and has subsequently become the standard in fast-pitch softball. In 1972, the firm produced the first one-piece aluminum bat and in the 1980s developed the first titanium bat. The titanium bat added 10% to hit distances over aluminum bats. The Copperhead ACX bat, shown here, is the first to use a dampening technology to remove the stinging sensation produced by strong ball impacts. A layer around the base, about 6in. from the bottom, of a piezo-electric material converts mechanical vibration into electrical current.

An LED red light at the bottom, when on, indicates that the piezo-electric material is working.

Vibration-control module

The key to this innovative concept is the placement of the dampener. According to the manufacturer, U.S. school ball players in a "double-blind" test preferred the Copperhead ACX over other high-end bats due to its reduction of sting to a batter's hands and a wider "sweet spot" (the area where the ball strikes the bat for the greatest travel distance).

Piezo dampener
Wiring harness
Bat
Wire slot
Electronic shunt circuit
LED red light

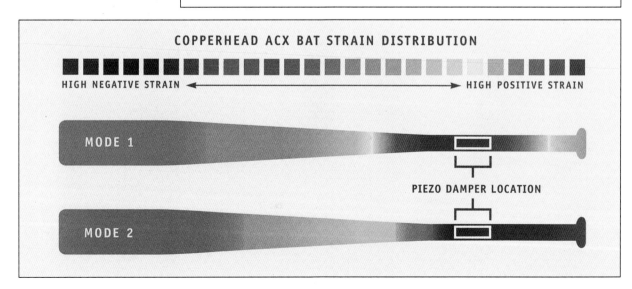

COPPERHEAD ACX BAT STRAIN DISTRIBUTION

HIGH NEGATIVE STRAIN ← → HIGH POSITIVE STRAIN

MODE 1

PIEZO DAMPER LOCATION

MODE 2

Dumb bells and jump rope

Designers: Asprey & Garrard staff
Manufacturer: Asprey & Garrard, London

The goldsmiths and jewelers Garrard was founded in London in 1721 and received its first royal appointment from Frederick, the Prince of Wales in 1753. For a time, its work was enviable enough to attract the attention of Odiot (the son of J.B.C. Odiot, the jeweler to Napoleon I) who was sent to study English craftsmanship at Garrard's. The firm was consolidated with the Goldsmiths' and Silversmiths' Company in 1952 and eventually with Asprey's. Even though some avant-garde items were produced in the 1950s, the company is still considered a conservative house. The items shown here are possibly more novelties than serious pieces of exercise equipment. The cost of the dumb bells is $5,760 (£3,600) and the jump rope $3,600 (£2,250).

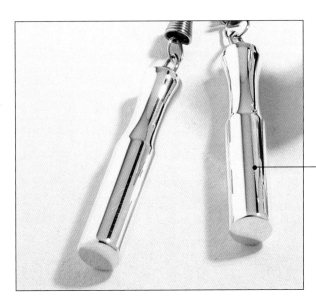

Handles of the jump rope are sterling silver.

The thongs of the jump rope are leather.

2.5kg dumb bells are solid sterling silver

Leather grips on the handlebar.

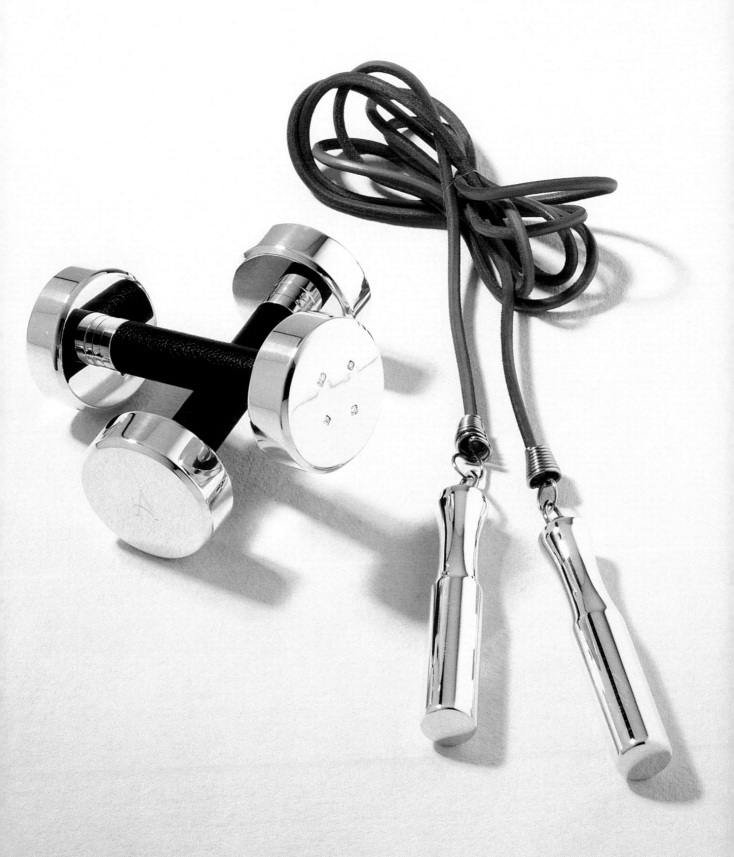

SPL Series fly rods and 3000 Series reels

Designers: Jerry Siem and Don Green
Manufacturer: Sage Manufacturing, Bainbridge Island, WA, U.S.A.
Date of design: 1998

Sage's 3000 Series fishing reels feature a large arbor design for faster line retrieval, more consistent drag as the line spools out, and reduced line coiling. The drag of a traditional small arbor reel increases as the diameter of the line of the spool decreases. The extra drag can sometimes break off fish or snap light tippets. Applying ultra-light graphite to the rod, the unique rod-and-reel configuration reduces the overall weight and favorably changes the balance point on the rod. The reels are available for 3-, 4-, 5-, 6-, and 8-weight lines, and the 8ft.9in. and 9ft. rods can be disassembled to fit into 23³/₄in. and 25in. tubes.

An SPL fly rod is made of a graphite-wrapped aluminum tube.

The rod is made through the use of a rolling machine (right), cello machine, and oven baking. The lightweight SPL medium-action rod is integrated with the reel and a special Quiet Taper™ fly line to reduce the overall weight and change the balance point.

The Sage 3000 Series reel (below) is machined from solid aluminum bars to precise tolerances and then anodized. The reel is strong yet lightweight and features a very smooth, adjustable click-drag to protect fine tippets. Fingertip control on the spool's palming rim controls large fish. The manufacturer claims that the reel, which is expensive, will last a lifetime. The drawing (below) demonstrates spool removal and the exploded drawing (below right) reveals the 23 separate parts that compose the spool.

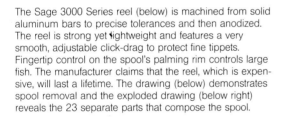

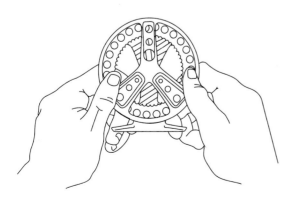

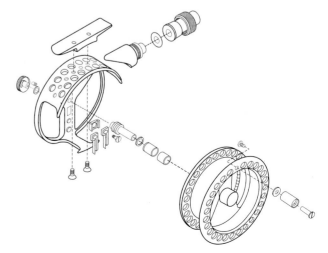

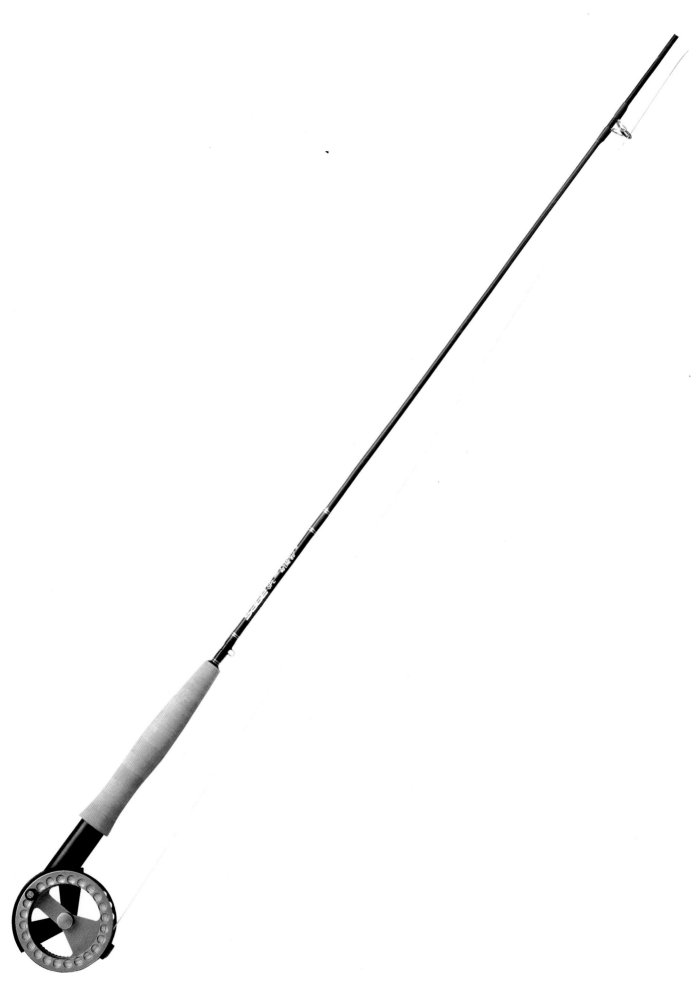

May Fly fly-fishing reel

Designer: Olivier Huynh
Manufacturer: Decathlon, Villeneuve d'Ascq, France
Date of design: 1995

Decathlon, selling directly to customers through its own retail stores, designs and manufactures some of the best sports equipment produced at reasonable prices. For example, about 3,000 of the reels shown here are sold annually for about $30 (£19) each. Decathlon's expansive manufacturing facilities are located in northern France, near Lille. Rather than calling on expensive, labor-intensive traditional materials, the May Fly reel is realized through the die-casting and injection-molding of aluminum and glass-fiber-impregnated polyamide. However, the assembly is by hand.

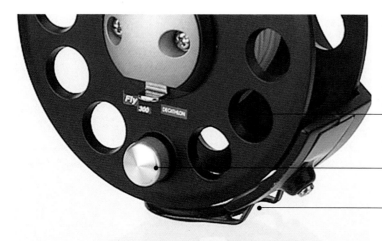

A ceramic ring is placed at the end of the line to prevent damage from lateral traction.

The reel holds 5–7m of line with a reserve.

The spool is demountable by means of a push button.

The powerful disk brake progressively applies pressure.

The reversible right- or left-handed spool is operated by a double crank to eliminate line breakage.

The May Fly is packaged in a neoprene container for protection during transport.

Continued on next page

May Fly fly-fishing reel

Fishing-reel factory.

Cutting tools for gears.

Silkscreen printing operation.

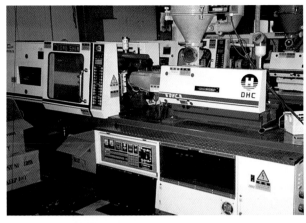

Plastic-injection press.

CNC (computer numeric control) cutting machine (left and below).

Workers assembling reels.

Woodpecker ice axe

Designers: Camp research-&-development staff
Manufacturer: Camp S.p.A., Premana (LC), Italy
Date of design: 1992

An indispensible tool for mountain climbing, the high-performance Woodpecker ice axe—no matter its amusing name—is a serious instrument designed for the kind of reliability and function demanded by extreme-mountaineering, particularly on ice falls and goulottes. A choice of three front picks and three back picks is available. The Woodpecker, whose features include four patents, is offered in four models of varying weights and sizes. Stemming from a need by Alpinists, the ice axe has evolved over the last 100 years and thus has no true inventor. The example here employs early, traditional forging methods, but the hands of blacksmiths have been replaced by machines that produce steel with fibers uniformly aligned for maximum strength in a one-piece head. No welding is involved.

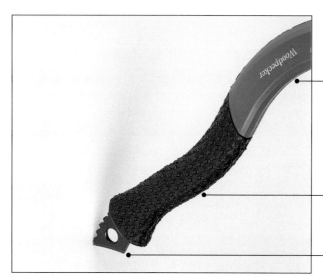

7075 aluminum alloy covered with du Pont's Hypalon.

Rubber covering molded by vulcanization.

Hot-pressed Ni-Cro-Mo (chromoly) steel.

The woven nylon and rubber strap is wrapped around a climber's wrist to prevent the axe from flying away.

Front, rear, and bottom pick elements are Ni-Cro-Mo steel, produced by a machine that makes rough blanks by a drop-forging press.

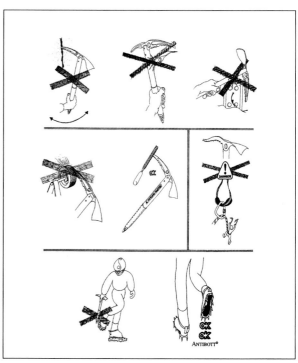

Instructions accompanying the product warn against improper use.

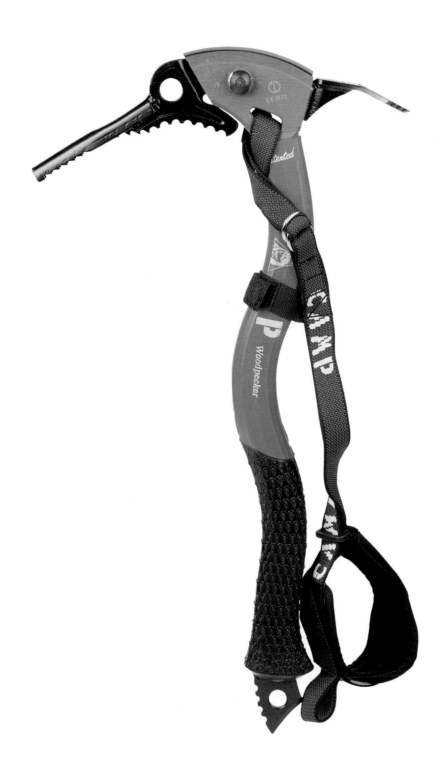

8

Attac carabiner

Designers: MM Design S.r.l.
Manufacturer: Oberalp Salewa S.p.A., Bolzano (VI), Italy
Date of design: 1996

Used for mountain-climbing routes with fixed ropes, the Attac carabiner (or snap-link) is special in that it offers a safety catch on the aperture to prevent the snap ring from opening when in use on difficult passages while making the safety catch immediately releasable. This solution called on tools in the building trade, particularly those used by window cleaners, where a reliable safety catch is indispensible. The designers paid particular attention to weight, mass, materials, usage, and various other dynamics. DAV, the German mountaineering association, has deemed the Attac ingenious and innovative.

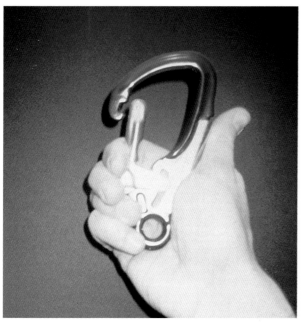

The designers called on testing and experts who work with the manufacturer to produce these prototypes in wood which were subsequently tested and refined.

Eloxid-finished aluminum alloy was chosen for its strength and lightweight characteristic. For the finished shape, a bar was hewn through various machining stages.

This highly simplified and stylized color rendering illustrates the closed (left) and open (right) positions.

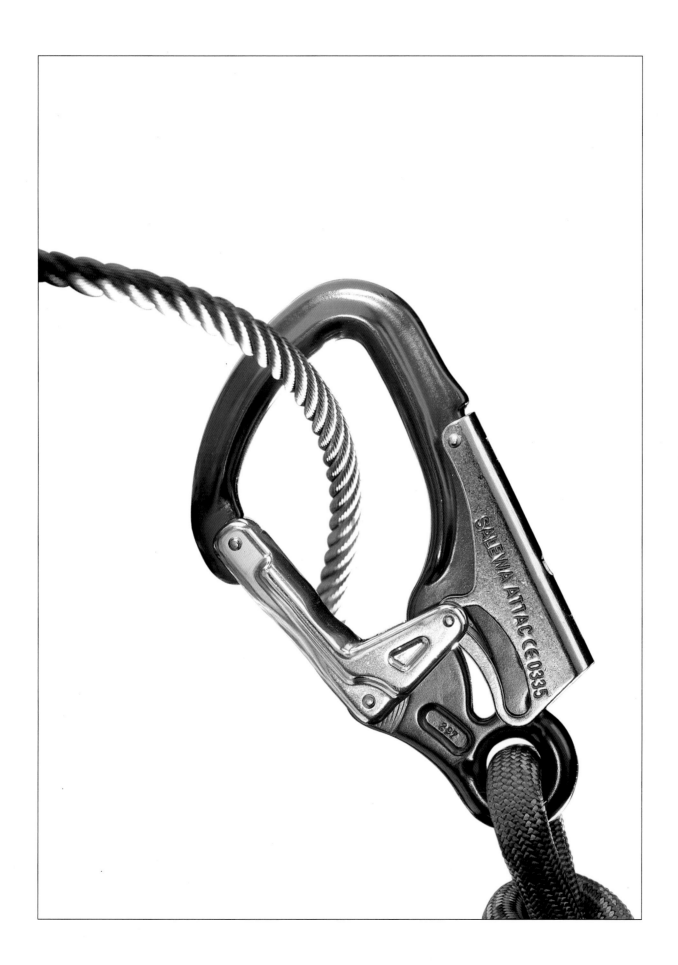

9

Fun Rang boomerang

Designer: Eric A. Darnell
Manufacturer: TopLine Toys, Sand City, CA, U.S.A.
Date of design: 1997

Even though boomerangs have a long history in Australia where they are the most refined and varied in the world, boomerang-type throwing sticks were found by Howard Carter in the tomb of Tutankhamen in 1927. And, in 1987, a 27,000-year-old woolly mammoth tusk, carved into the shape of a boomerang, was found in Poland. An interest in boomerang throwing remains to today. Eric A. Darnell, an international boomerang champion, who developed the inexpensive three-bladed example shown here, holds the record for boomerang flight time at one minute and 44.87 seconds, achieved on 21 September 1997.

Injection-molding machine (left) into which the dies (below) are fitted.

The top (core) and bottom (cavity) sides of the die (below) produce three-bladed boomerangs and a wave boomerang with each injection process. Liquid plastic is forced into the mold, under high heat and pressure, through small tubes.

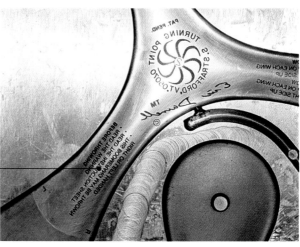

So that the image on the plastic surface of the boomerang will be readable, it is etched as a negative on the core side of the die's surface.

Continued on next page

Fun Rang boomerang

In the bottom section of the die (above), tubular extensions reveal the route the injected material travels to reach the hollow areas where the boomerangs are formed. The tubular extensions are broken away and smoothed over on the final pieces.

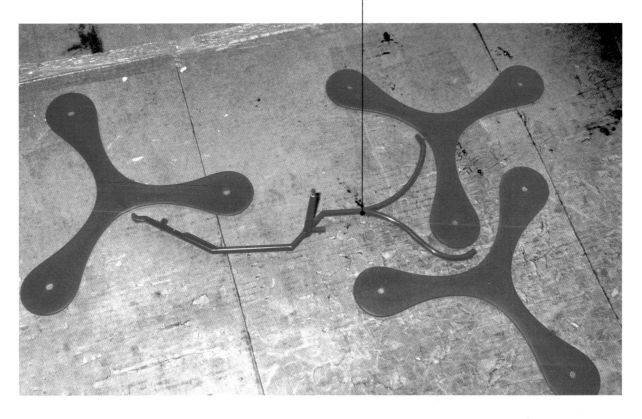

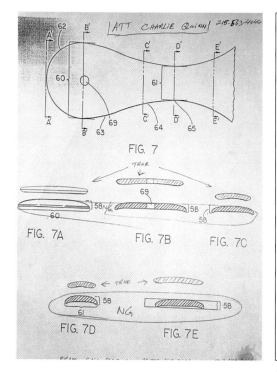

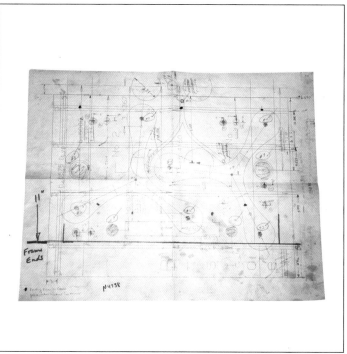

Preliminary sketches (an example at left) by the designer must be eventually developed into the kind of precise drawings (an example at right) necessary to make molds.

Instructions on the backside of the packaging informs the user of tuning procedures and methods of throwing for best results.

Firesole Metalwood golf clubs

Designers: Philippe Besnard and Jim Sieleman
Manufacturer: Taylor Made Golf Co., Carlsbad, CA, U.S.A.
Date of design: 1998

Players of golf, a difficult game to master, need all the assistance that manufacturers of clubs and balls can offer to improve their performance. Gone are the days of wooden clubs and inexpensive prices. High-tech versions, like the example here, are configured to a specific weight and to strike the ball at hopefully a precise point, thereby sending balls to various angles of loft. The shaft must provide a certain flex. The Firesole Metalwood clubs are composed of a wide range of materials that include titanium, tungsten steel, a graphite composite, rubber, and epoxy glue. Approximately 500,000 Firesole Metalwood clubs have been produced at a cost to players of about $480 (£300) each, and a set includes a number of club-angle types.

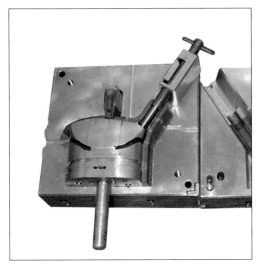

The pins of the top section (lower right) of the two-part mold are inserted into the bottom section, and titanium is injected into the hollow through the trough seen at top left side of the right half of the mold.

Mold and core.

View of the sole.

View of the crown that, when finished and attached to the shaft, results in a club of about 45in. long overall.

Continued on next page

Firesole Metalwood golf clubs

The body is made of titanium. A weight plug in the sole of the head is made of tungsten steel. The shaft is made of a graphite composite. The grip of the shaft (not shown here) is made of rubber.

The head is composed of vacuum-formed investment-cast titanium, arc-welded in an inert atmosphere. The tungsten-steel weight plug is pressure-molded through powder metallurgy. The weight plug is joined to the body via machining and riveting. Finally, hand grinding, polishing, automatic painting, and hand-fill painting of the engraving occurs.

The shaft is a pre-impregnated graphite composite that is hand laid up, centerless sanded, painted, and printed.

The grip is injection-molded rubber and is glued to the shaft.

Assembly procedure: Laser-guided manual grip is applied at the point-of-application with an epoxy glue. The epoxy is conductively and locally cured. The final product is cleaned and polished by hand.

Both extensive research into technology, engineering, and materials (below) and intuitive investigation contribute to creating a golf club that will propel a ball forward with a certain loft to the place where intended. This varies, of course, according to the club-angle type and a player's expertise.

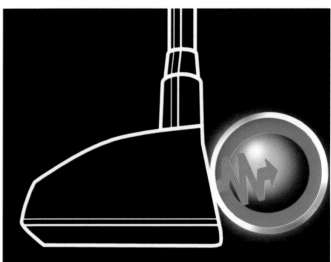

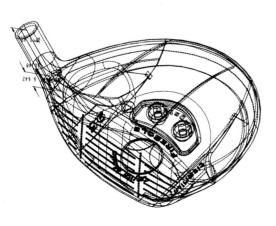

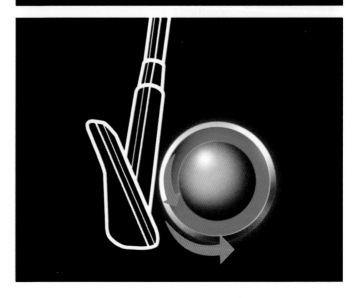

Vehicles

Eko® Snow-Comet 100 and 120 toboggans

Designer: Erich Kohler
Manufacturer: Formenbau GmbH, Trachslau, Switzerland, for
Eko® Swiss Made, Boswil, Switzerland
Dates: 1998 (Eko®-Snow-Comet 100) and 1999 (Eko®-Snow-Comet 120)

The designer and manufacturer have produced an inexpensive
line of children's products in a colorful plastic, including simple sleds,
skis, ski poles, snow shoes, and shovels. The steerable Snow-Comet
toboggans (in either 100- or 120cm-long models shown here) can be
kept on track, safely and effectively maneuvered on racy, straight, or
winding courses, and ridden by adults.

The Snow-Comet 100 (100cm long) can
accommodate children or older adolescents.

The Snow-Comet 120 (120cm long) can
accommodate 2 children or 1 adult.

The brake, screwed to the body in 4 places, is operable by one hand.

Except for the metal brake handle and steering column, all parts are polyethylene. An optional cushion (not shown) makes the seat more comfortable.

Steering is made possible by the steering wheel which rotates the ridged sled on the underside of the front end.

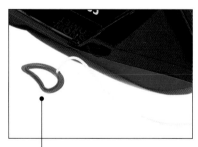

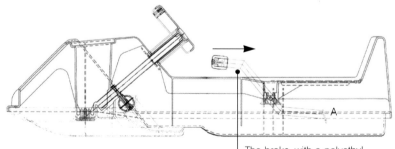

The toboggan can be pulled by a plastic handle and rope.

The brake, with a polyethylene knob, is firmly attached to the body in 4 places. A broad metal plate (A) at the end of the "L"-shaped lever digs into soft as well as icy surfaces.

Directional sled

Designer: Benoît Vignot
Manufacturer: Benoît Vignot, Paris, France.
Date of design: 1998

The Directional sled is a whole new concept for mountain sledding. Through the use of high-tech plastics and composites, designer Benoît Vignot was able to combine elasticity, plasticity, and strength with flexibility and lightness. The sled's innovations include a tension-frame shape, a saddle-type configuration, and a comfortable, flexible base that permits directional steering. Strings hold the one-piece frame tautly.

In action on the slopes.

Extensive modeling of flex and geometry via computer technology was conducted. The example below is one of many.

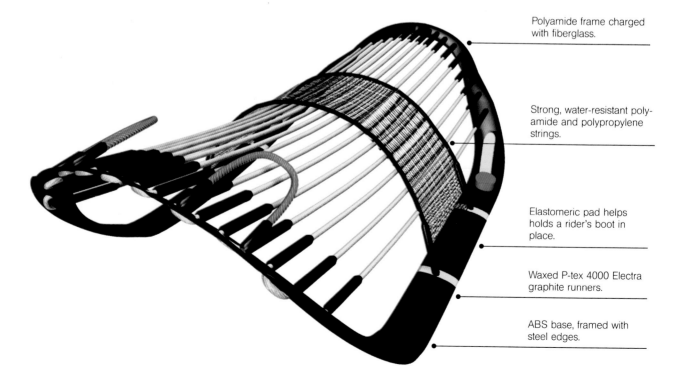

Polyamide frame charged with fiberglass.

Strong, water-resistant polyamide and polypropylene strings.

Elastomeric pad helps holds a rider's boot in place.

Waxed P-tex 4000 Electra graphite runners.

ABS base, framed with steel edges.

13

Ina Zone 230 kayak

Designer: Graham Mackereth
Manufacturer: Pyranha Mouldings Ltd, Runcorn, Cheshire, Great Britain
Date: 1999

The use of materials, technology, and design of kayak production has rapidly changed over the past decades. The sport of freestyle kayaking, which has grown in popularity, has encouraged the use of advanced plastics technology for the production of stronger, lighter, and generally shorter models. Examples of this new production, like the one shown here, are more maneuverable than the awkward fiberglass versions of the 1970s and '80s. Used by the best paddlers worldwide, the less experienced can easily handle the Ina Zone 230 kayak in friendly water.

Graphics are being pre-applied to the surface of a boat still in the mold.

Bottom view of the new form for freestyling. The kayak can be used in more turbulent waters and will facilitate amazing moves. Some of the world's top paddlers are able to perform aerial moves off huge waves and stoppers.

A boat shell (left), molded in metallocene (a high-density polyethylene), is ready for curing in the oven.

"Shoc Bloc" foot rest.

Four sectional pairs of side padding protect a paddler from high-impact shocks.

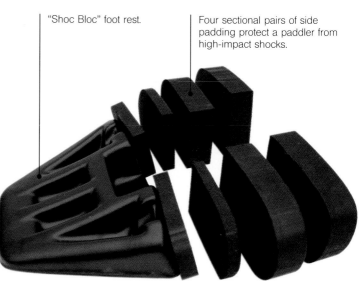

Lookin bicycle saddles

Designers: Selle Royal staff
Manufacturer: Selle Royal S.p.A., Pozzeleone (VI), Italy
Date of design: 1997

The comfort and healthful attributes offered by the bicycle saddles of Selle Royal have been realized through the use of an advanced gel that the firm calls Royalgel. The substance is a product with intriguing bio-ergonomic properties. The various models of Selle Royal saddles feature different distributions of the gel padding depending on the riding positions that range from racing or mountain riding to trekking and touring and the sex of the user. However, some models are appropriate for either sex.

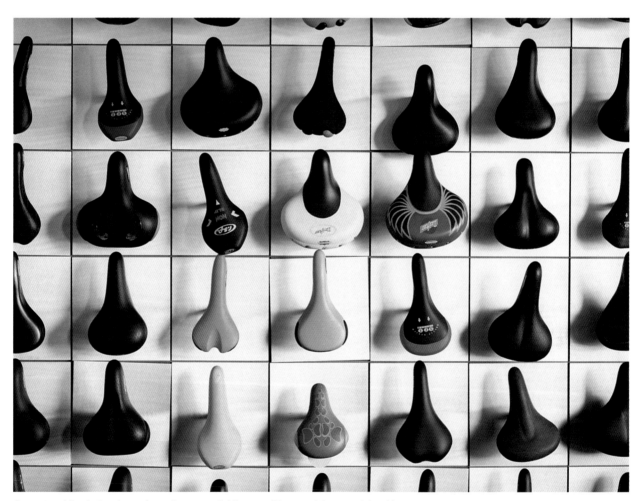

Correct saddle choice depends on the types of riding conditions and the sex of the rider.

MTB saddles: For mountain or racing use when a cyclist's back is bent forward to an angle of not more than 30° and when great pressure is exerted on the entire genital zone, the front section of the saddle is padded with a greater amount of gel than in other models.

Trekking saddles: For trekking use when the angle of a cyclist's back is between 30° and 60° and when pressure shifts to the ischio-genital area, the gel is distributed uniformly over the entire saddle surface.

Touring saddles: For touring use when a cyclist's back is almost erect or at an angle from 60° to 90° and when most of the body pressure is on the ischial zone, the gel is shifted to the back.

Continued on next page

14

Lookin bicycle saddles

A robot works on molds as they rotate on the factory carousel.

A workman removes a saddle seat from a mold on the carousel.

Workers on the finishing line.

Saddle cover being positioned.

The handmade cover is fitted to the substrate.

Finishing.

Resistance testing of a saddle.

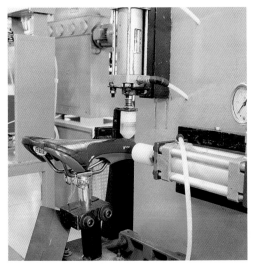
Clamp test.

Elastomer-compression test.

Ultra-violet rays test for color fading.

15

Ribbon bicycle handlebar tapes

Designers: Cinelli staff
Manufacturer: Cinelli Division, Gruppo S.p.A., Caleppio de Setiala (MI), Italy
Date of design: 1995 (cork) and 1997 (stripe)

Handlebar tapes are an integral component of bicycles and indispensible in competition racing. Cinelli tapes are a mixture of polyurethane and cork. When wrapped around a handlebar, they absorb perspiration from the hands and ensure a safe, comfortable grip. The addition of cork in handlebar tape has provided benefits unrealized before now. This group of tapes by Cinelli allows cyclists to personalize their machines. The handlebars on which the tapes are demonstrated here are, of course, Cinelli's own.

Cinelli's Ribbon tape, made of polyurethane with a high natural-cork content, insures a tight grip and absorbs hand sweat. Color fading is retarded by the use of vat-dyed, not surprinted, material. This particular Cinelli product has encouraged blatant imitations.

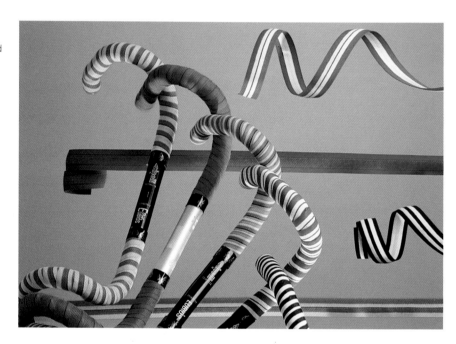

Cinelli's Cork tape in non-fading solid colors (see facing page) is available in a 12-color palette (right).

Each tape section is about 1,800mm long.

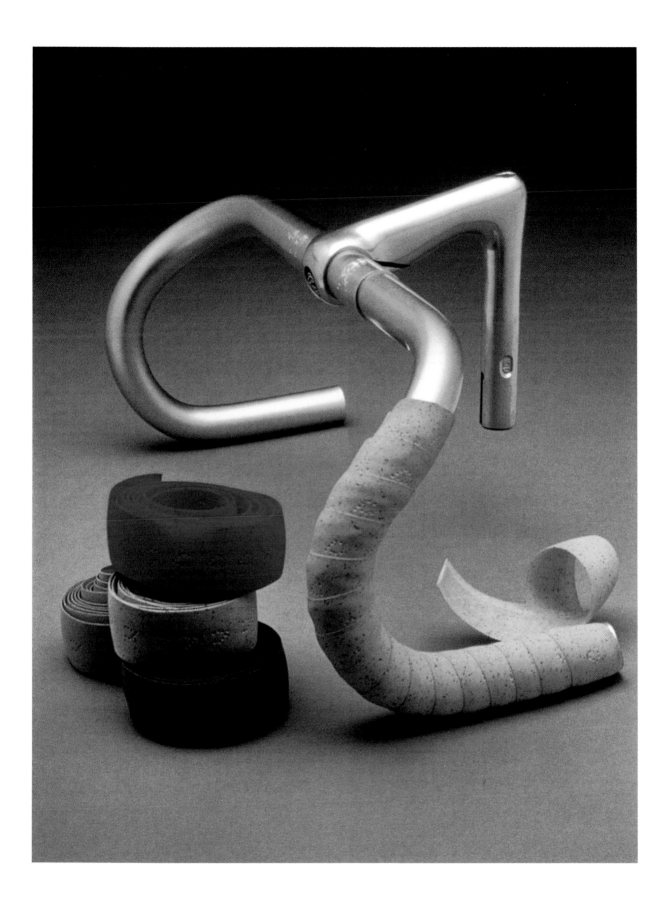

Lobo DH 1000 downhill bicycle

Designers: Jim Busby and GT Bicycles staff
Manufacturer: GT Bicycles, Inc., Santa Ana, CA, U.S.A.
Date of design: 1999

The manufacturer of this bicycle and others in its line claims to take technology seriously rather than make gimmicks for the youth market. Toward this dogged pursuit, the firm spent $2,700,000 (£1,800,000) on research and development in 1997 alone. The prices of its vehicles range from $4,400 (£2,300) for the Lobo shown here to $390 (£240) for its aluminum Aggressor model. The Lobo, available in small, medium, and large sizes, was built for fast competition racing over rough terrain. However, the bike no doubt appeals to amateur afficionados who can afford the price. Designed for extra-long travel with good turnability, Lobo's features include an ultra-sturdy frame, disc brakes, reinforced forks, and other examples of the finest components available today.

Rock Shox Coupe Deluxe pull shock with a rebound and compression-dampening adjuster. The 6in. give of the rear suspension resists squatting under power.

Avid 2.0 brake levers with a speed dial. Atomic riser handlebar. Forged and machined aluminum billet stem. Pro Grip grips, made in Italy for GT.

SDG Big Boy saddle with a Kevlar cover.

6061–16 aluminum front triangle.

Rock Shox Boxxer Hydracoil DH fork.

Mavic D321, 32H rims.

Shimano Super Narrow 9-speed chain

Shimano DX pedals.

Shimano XTR derailleur.

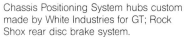

Chassis Positioning System hubs custom made by White Industries for GT; Rock Shox rear disc brake system.

Lobo DH 1000 downhill bicycle

The Trunion shock mount (right) on the Lobo allows for the bottom bracket height, the bike's handling characteristics, and the overall center of gravity which can be tuned for terrain, use, and ride preference.

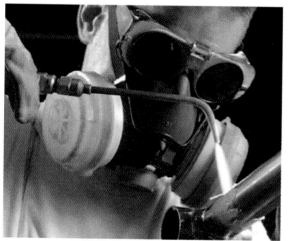

GT's i-drive independently suspended crank.

Eccentric BB in the crank shaft.

Main pivot.

Rock Shox front disc-brake system.

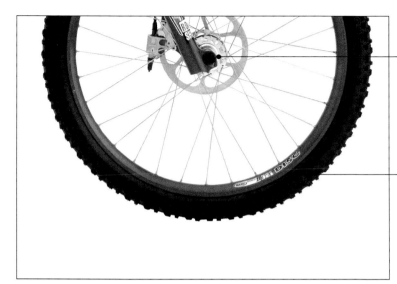

White Industries front hubs with 20mm through axle.

Michelin Wild Gripper DH, 26 x 22, wire head tires.

In use on a course of the professional downhill circuit.

17

Series M Model XC/2 cross-country bicycle

Designer: J.M. Seynhaeve
Manufacturer: Decathlon, Villeneuve d'Ascq, France
Date of design: 1998

Serving sports enthusiasts as well as professional athletes, Decathlon
not only sells a wide array of equipment and clothing by various manufacturers through its own chain of retail stores but also employs a
staff of designers and produces its own sophisticated sporting goods.
Decathlon's XC/2 is a training and competition bicycle intended for
cross-country use. Available in four sizes, the extremely lightweight
vehicle that is subjected to stringent testing incorporates advanced
materials and technology.

All Decathlon bikes must pass demanding tests performed at the technical center at Villeneuve d'Ascq.

Cabinet where a frame is being powder painted.

A device for testing the resistance of the
paint finish to scratching and chipping from
impacts.

Continued on next page

Series M Model XC/2 cross-country bicycle

The overall weight is 10.9kg.

The aluminum parts are protected against oxidation. Anticorrosive polyurethane paint, like that used in the automobile industry, is applied to other parts to offer resistance to chemical breakdown, discoloration caused by ultra-violet rays, and flying gravel.

Rock Shox SID XC fork (pump included) offering 63mm rebound and up to 1,350kg shock.

24/34/46 XTR–12/34 9-speed chain wheel.

Shimano XTR crankcase.

Choice of Time Atac or Shimano M535 pedals.

Front and rear XTR V-brakes operated in progressive-force increments.

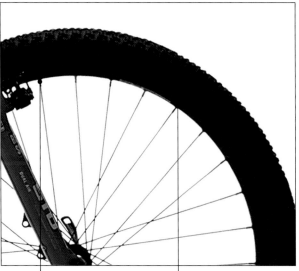

Welded frame
sections.

Mavic X517 rims of
Maxtal aluminum.

Choice of
Hutchinson
Python or
Caméléon tires.

Flite Kevlar vanadium saddle,
to offer comfort on descend-
ing passages.

Columbus Altec[2]
frame

18

Soft Machine bicycle

Designers: Cinelli technical department in collaboration with Alessandra
"Titi" Cusatelli and Guido Morozzi
Manufacturer: Cinelli Division, Gruppo S.p.A., Caleppio di Setiala (MI), Italy
Date of design: 1998

The shape-butted construction of this bike was developed according to
stress-analysis studies. Made by a renowned bicycle manufacturer, the
Soft Machine is extremely light and features the kind of resistance that an
oval-tube frame can offer. The tubing was developed to provide rigidity
coupled with safety under extreme racing conditions. Columbus's production is considered the *ne plus ultra* of bicycle tubing.

The tig-welded frame is Columbus Altec[2] aluminum alloy 7000 Series. The bike parts are manually assembled.

Cinelli Grammo head stem, 3T Pro Bar handlebar, Shimano XT seat post, FI'ZI:K Pavé saddle.

High-quality Italian-made Columbus tubing is the choice of numerous competition-quality bicycle manufacturers, like Cinelli.

Rock Shox Judy XC forks, Shimano XT mix groupset, and Shimano XT 9V gear.

A non-destructive eddy-current testing device (above) at Columbus provides ultra-sonic inspec-tion and rotomat testing.

The frame is painted micalized black, and reflective decals are applied.

Columbus's Magnaflux device (left) detects superficial defects that may occur in the tubing.

Downhill Pro, Cruiser, and City scooters

Designer: Walther Steindlegger
Manufacturer: BlauWerk K.E.G., Vienna, Austria.
Dates: 1992 (City), 1994 (Downhill Pro and Cruiser)

Scooters are normally thought of as vehicles for children's play. However, the scooters, or Sidewalkers, by BlauWerk are intended for adults with all the special high-tech features and fittings found on sophisticated competition bicycles. Various models, in addition to the examples here, are available in a range of prices and for different uses.

The model shown here is the Downhill Pro. Even though conceived as a scooter, it is, in fact, a new sports bike in the form of a racing machine.

Length 193cm
H-bar height 106cm
Weight 13.5kg

Michelin Wild Gripper 26 x 20 tire.

Marzocchi Bomber Z1 suspension fork.

Mavic D521 SAI, aluminum 26in. rim.

Monotube 50.8mm frame, powder-coated finish.

Magura HS44 disc brake or Magura HS33 Raceline.

Continued on next page

Downhill, Cruiser, and City scooters

The Cruiser (below) is the first scooter to offer 25 gears, and includes a kick stand, bell, basket, and fender.
Cromoly/Hi-Ten frame, chromium plated
26in. steel rims
Cantilever brake
Length 187cm
H-bar height 105cm
Weight 13kg

The City (below) is the least expensive Blau-Werk model, also available in a chromium-plated limited edition.
Cromoly frame, powder coated
26in. aluminum rims
V-brake
Length 182cm
H-bar height 105cm
Weight 11.5kg

Bodywear

Avant 55 backpack

Designers: Olivier Loup and others
Manufacturer: Lafuma S.A., Anneyron, France
Date of design: 1998

This manufacturer's number and variations of appurtenances used by
trekkers is extensive; its products include tent-floor pads, eyeglass cases,
ponchos, luggage, papooses, and backpacks. The example here illustrates
the innovative principles incorporated into Lafuma's range of backpacks.
An original concept, the sack can be opened quickly up the middle. The
system also offers ventilation, easy adjustment of the straps, and other
innovations that include highly functional and ergonomic features.

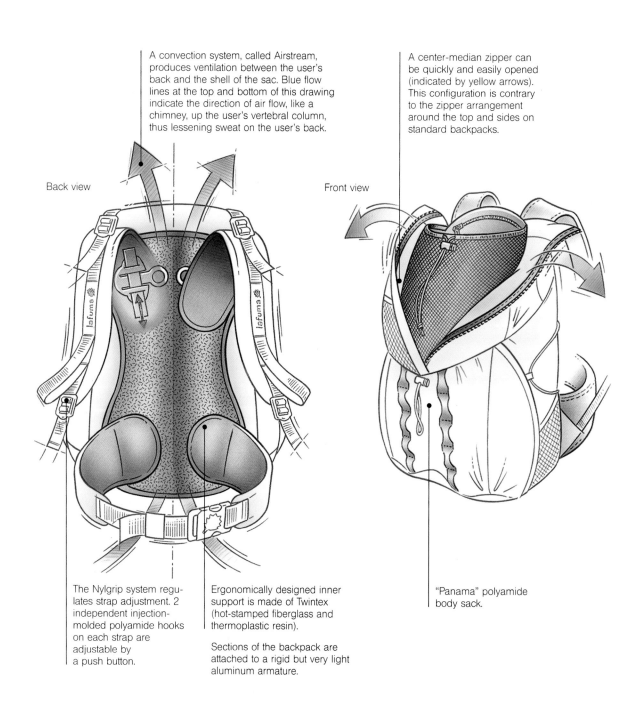

A convection system, called Airstream,
produces ventilation between the user's
back and the shell of the sac. Blue flow
lines at the top and bottom of this drawing
indicate the direction of air flow, like a
chimney, up the user's vertebral column,
thus lessening sweat on the user's back.

A center-median zipper can
be quickly and easily opened
(indicated by yellow arrows).
This configuration is contrary
to the zipper arrangement
around the top and sides on
standard backpacks.

Back view

Front view

The Nylgrip system regu-
lates strap adjustment. 2
independent injection-
molded polyamide hooks
on each strap are
adjustable by
a push button.

Ergonomically designed inner
support is made of Twintex
(hot-stamped fiberglass and
thermoplastic resin).

Sections of the backpack are
attached to a rigid but very light
aluminum armature.

"Panama" polyamide
body sack.

21

Metaltex fabric and clothing

Designers: Castelli staff
Manufacturer: Castelli S.p.A., Rosate (MI), Italy
Date of design: 1996–97

A revolutionary new textile, Metaltex was used for the uniforms of the Italian cycling team at the Summer Olympic Games at Atlanta in 1966. A proprietary method employs a special vacuum process to coat silver particles onto an elastic fabric. The material becomes breathable and helps to regulate body temperature.

Castelli's Micronet on upper parts of the outfit are combined with reflective Metaltex elsewhere to offer optimal body thermo-regulation.

All elements of the outfit are antibacterially and antiwrinkle treated. The vacuum-processed silver fabric is both aesthetically attractive and photoreflective. Silver micro particles are bombarded onto the fabric without affecting its elastic and transpirant qualities.

The pad, set by flat-seam construction, is anatomically cut to reduce the weight and excess of the material while providing comfort and protection. The pad layers are constructed of perforated Alcathara "leather" with an 8mm antivibration foam that eliminates compression even after extended sitting. The pad has a split back so that the biker can achieve a correct position on the saddle.

A size "large" jersey weighs only 85g compared to 170g for traditional polyester. At a temperature of 35–40°C (95–104°F) and humidity of 90%, an athlete's body heat will remain constant and physiologically regulated.

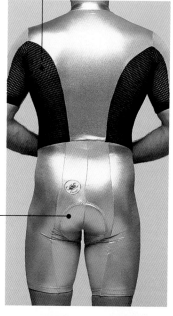

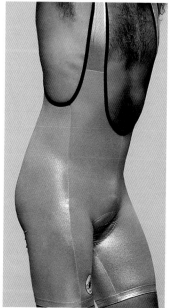

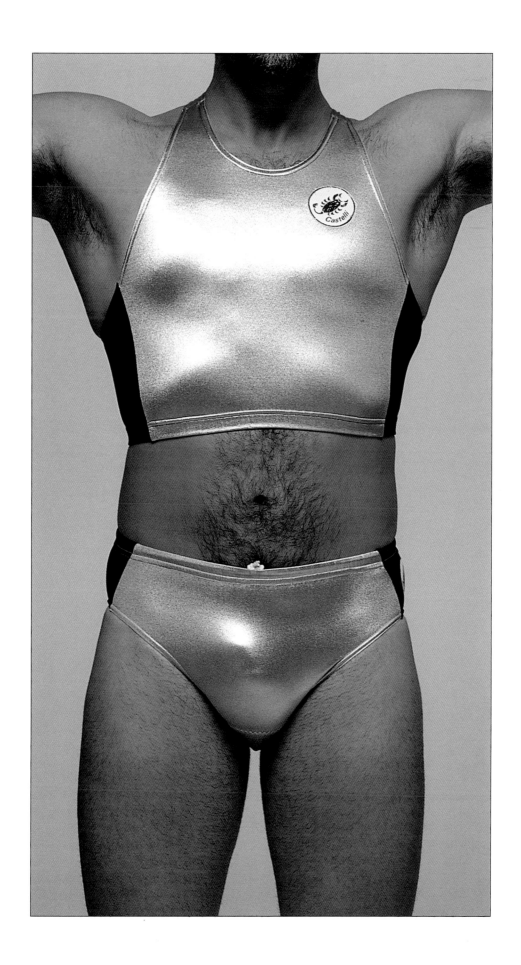

22

Electric Lady fabric and clothing

Designer: Paola Pezzo
Manufacturer: Castelli S.p.A., Rosate (MI), Italy
Date of design: 1999

At a time not long ago, sports clothing specially designed for female competition athletes was scarce. For Castelli, mountain biker Paola Pezzo has designed a collection of jerseys, vests, shorts, pants, and tops that offers high style and technological benefits—a combination of fashion and function. Pezzo gives her approval of the garments only after she herself has tested them under competitive conditions. An example from one of the collections, Electric Lady, is shown here.

Specially finished
elasticized Lycra fiber
by du Pont.

A colored pattern is printed on the external weft in a micro-octagonal slough that has the appearance of glittering snake skin.

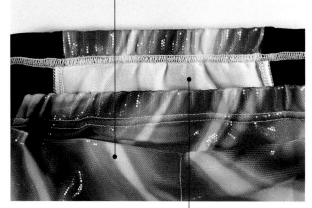

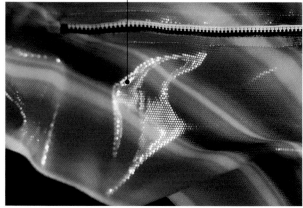

Backside of the jersey
fabric is smooth.

Competition mountain-bike cyclist Paola Pezzo on the course.

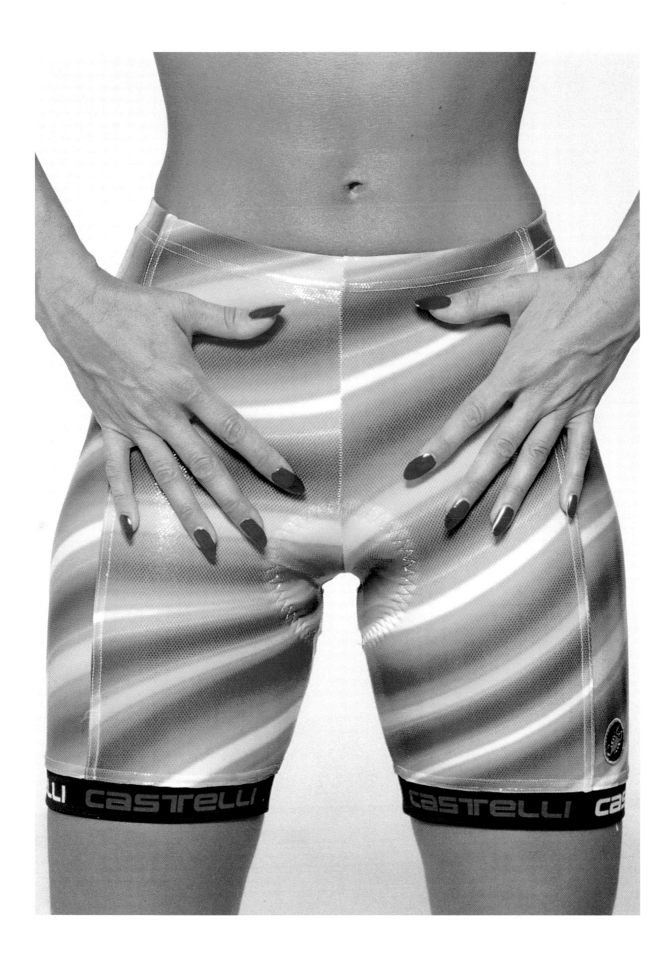

Animal wet suit

Designers: Bradford Bissell and Stephen Peart (designers), Mike Gifford
(computer programmer), Carl Schwarz (material developer), Vent Design
Associates, Campbell, CA, and Pat O'Neill, O'Neill Inc.
Manufacturer: O'Neill Inc., San Francisco, CA, (suit); Rubatex Corporation,
Bedford, VA, U.S.A. (material)
Date of design: 1989

This intentionally intimidating wet suit is the result of the happy marriage of function and the manufacturer to aesthetics and the designers. In the 1950s, Jack
O'Neill, the owner of a family-run surf shop in California, began studies of human
physiology as it pertained to the performance of wet suits. His research centered
on advanced-materials technology and how it might be applied to synthetic rubber. The eventual material of choice in 1952 was neoprene. Even so, the Animal
is the result of adjusting a neoprene sheath to human-body movement, solving
the problem of stress points, and reducing the weight as much as possible.

Illustrations of the behavior of
neoprene, a closed-cell sponge-
like synthetic rubber.

Neoprene in a relaxed state.

Neoprene in an expanded state.

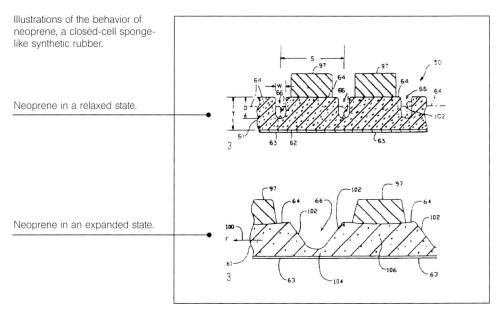

Drawings (overlapped and in
color here) accompanying the
U.S.A. patent application by
Vent Design.

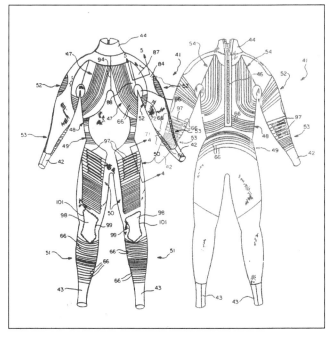

Continued on next page

Animal wet suit

Expensive molding equipment, that produces only 2 wet suits at a time, was developed according to Mike Gifford's computer-generated drawings. In addition, a waterproof zipper and detachable parts (sleeves, legs, and hood) were integral to the design solution. New techniques and processes for molding, cutting, connecting, and seam shaping included CNC (computer numeric control) cutting, laser machinery and special glues. The result is a suit 20% lighter and 27% more flexible than wet suits of the same material thickness.

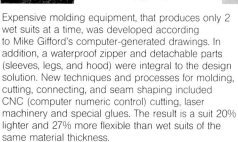

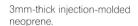

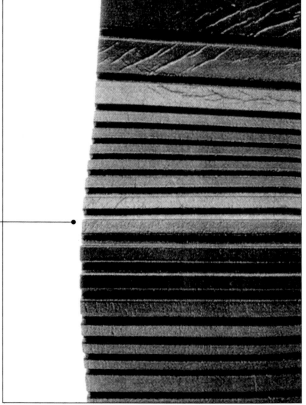

3mm-thick injection-molded neoprene.

The grooves molded into neoprene, an easy-to-process-and-wear substance, can be seen in this amplified view. Its ability to insulate is beholden to its thickness. Thicker is warmer but cumbersome. By incorporating furrows at the high-flex areas of the lower back, thighs, and chest, the material will protect a surfer against cold water while offering maximum pliancy.

Boards—Skis

Beta racing skis

Designers: Design Continuum Italia
Manufacturer: Atomic GmbH, Altenmarkt, Austria
Date of design: 1997

A design by an Italian studio for an Austrian client, the fast and dynamic Beta skis are built for precise giant-slalom competition racing. They feature asymmetrical side cuts for carving at top speeds. But their most obvious attribute may lie in the graphics. The Formula One checkered-flag motif was the main inspiration behind the graphics, intended to remind a potential customer of the competitive-racing milieu. Sales increased when Atomic sponsored the Austrian national team during the 1997–98 season and ran television commercials. Design Continuum's matching designs for the Atomic Carv X boots (see pages 117–120) and poles augments the visual recognition.

The profile of the Beta—side cuts for turning at high speeds—provides harmonic flex and smooth, secure edge gripping along the entire length of the skis.

The bold graphic vocabulary is intended to emphasize the new technology of the Beta, radius of the cut, new product name, manufacturer's name, and ski length. The graphics are recognizable, even when the skis are moving at high speeds.

Cubix 3X Skating skis

Designers: Pasi Järvinen and Juha Kosonen, Creadesign Oy;
Product Development Group, Karhu Sporting Goods Oy
Manufacturer: Karhu Sporting Goods Oy, Kitee, Finland
Date of design: 1993–95

A new approach to ski design, the Cubix 3X Skating ski is a self-bearing monocoque structure with a twist-rigid elliptical surface; the binding side is essentially flat. The construction of the body, a rigid skeletal configuration, appreciably eliminates weight. The skis are best used when snow is wet. Another version (not shown) has been developed for dry-snow conditions. The advanced materials used in the construction of the Cubix 3X Skating ski include a plastic foam (for the fill), carbon fiber, sintered (beaten without melting) polyurethane, epoxy resin, and graphite.

Detail of the underside of a 1994 prototype. The dimple acts as a soft directional fin.

A computer-generated illustration, drawn in 1994.

Protective cushion tip.

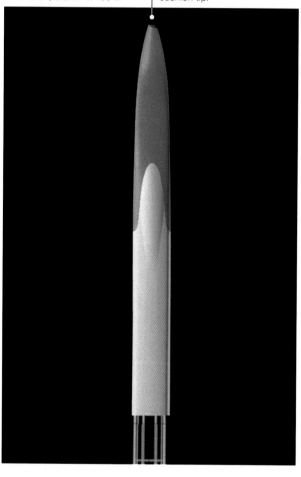

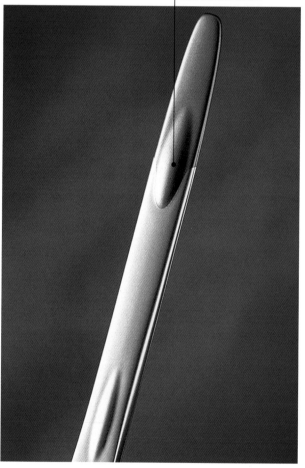

The finishing process is accomplished by milling and grinding. Construction is realized by a compactor and by compression and steel molds. The surface is printed by a sublimation process. The Skating skis are available in 160, 170, 180, 188, and 196cm lengths, 44mm wide.

Sublimated polyamide underside surface.

Integrated fiber structure.

Acrylic-foam core.

Laminated reinforcement.

F-base graphite plastic.

26

Race snowboard binding

Designers: MM Design S.r.l.
Manufacturer: Burton Snowboards, Innsbruck, Austria
Date of design: 1994

Italian studio MM Design has designed a range of sports equipment
for a number of clients, including Burton, a leader in the field. (See
pages 82–83.) Burton's Race binding shown here is able to transmit
a snowboarder's erratic impulses and abrupt movements to the snowboard itself. Intended for competition use, as its name implies, the
device was made possible by the use of the kind of high-resistance
materials that handles excessive stress. Compare this interpretation
with the binding by the same designers for another manufacturer
(pages 82–83).

A maquette of the table (or platform) in painted wood.

A maquette in wood and metal of the cover and pre-
existing clamping lever used on another Burton binding.

The stiffened the
injection-molded
ABS cover, it is
attached to the
central tie plate.

The aluminum tie plate is
screwed to the table.

The clamping lever, designed a month before the Race binding for
Burton's Reactor snowboard, is applicable for other snowboards.

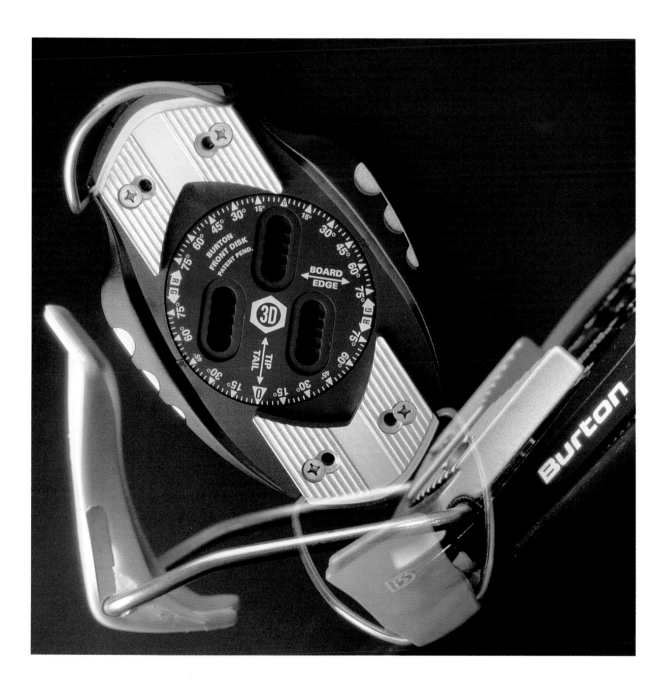

27

Easy-Go touring ski binding

Designers: MM Design S.r.l.
Manufacturer: Silvretta GmbH, Karlsfeld-Rotschwaige, Germany
Date of design: 1996

Silvretta produces top-of-the-line products for Alpine skiing, continuously encouraging new ideas and testing traditional and advanced materials. MM Design was commissioned to redesign a pre-existing, functioning, and tested prototype of a touring binding. The staff of MM Design worked with various specialists, including the Kunststoff Zentrum of Leipzig on the plastics and the Technologische Universität of Dresden on kinematic-motion mechanisms and dynamic tests of the finished elements. The assignment required quick results. The choices of materials had to satisfy resistance to cold temperatures, mechanical stress, high impact, and other factors. Compare this binding with the Burton version by the same designers (pages 80–81).

The system of heel lift on ascent and clamping on descent was devised with an eye to aesthetics and ergonomics. The mechanism, streamlined to give the appearance of lightness, can be operated by hand, ski poles, or sticks. A quick, lateral safety release engages during a fall but is easy to reset, particularly in fresh, deep snow.

Preliminary sketch.

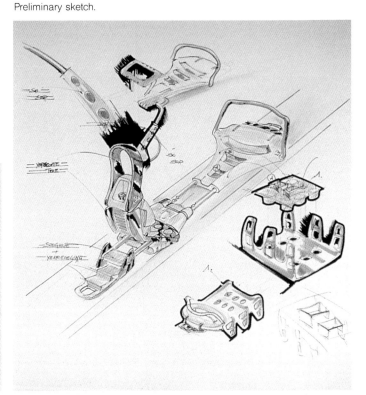

Maquette in wood.

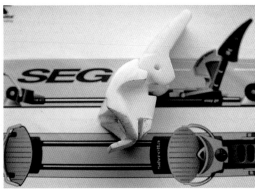

Renderings and prototypes.

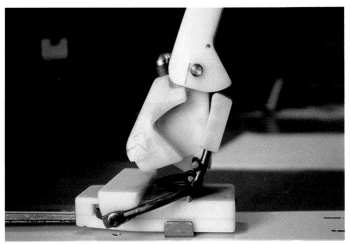

Nylon and metal prototype is shown here. The final production mechanism was made of du Pont's Delrin, steel, and carbon fiber.

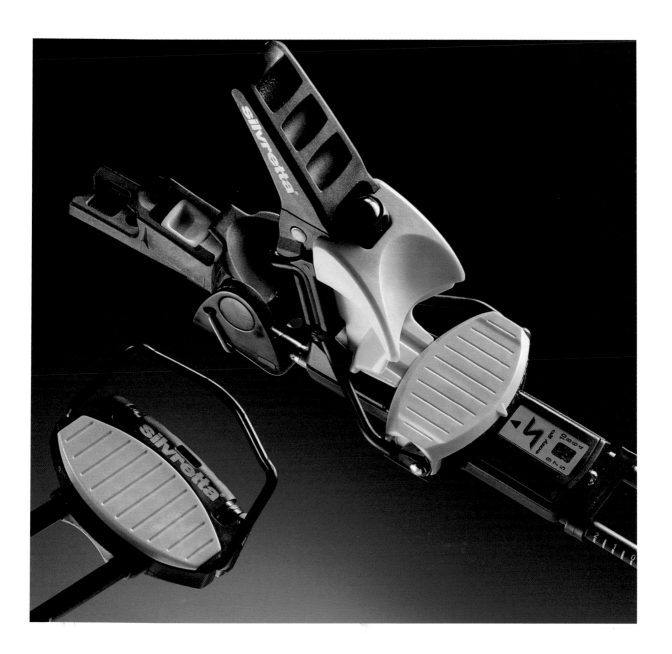

Skateboard

Designer: Stephen Peart
Manufacturer: Santa Cruz, Santa Cruz, CA, U.S.A.
Date of design: 1995

A new approach to skateboard design was spurred by the possibility of creating an example in a molded thermoplastic material—one that would meet or exceed the performance of existing wood designs and still be sold at a reasonable price. The project was further encouraged by the scarcity of sugar maplewood (see page 87–90). Since skateboarders are young and highly demanding, the new proprietary material (Nuwood) had to satisfy the flexibility, weight, and feel of wood and withstand harsh treatment. The romance with traditional materials had to be overcome. To the purchaser of a board, the manufacturer provides a voucher for its return, for whatever reasons, for recycling and use in making another board.

Nuwood, a newly formulated plastic, offers the benefits of wood while increasing wood's strength and flexibility and offering resistance to scraping and other damage. And, like fibrous plant material, the malleable matrix ages—a characteristic unique in polymer blends.

The body is Nuwood, an injection-molded recycled post-industrial Nylon 66 that is combined with short carbon fibers which are positioned lengthwise like wood grains to form a micro-cellular, unidirectional matrix.

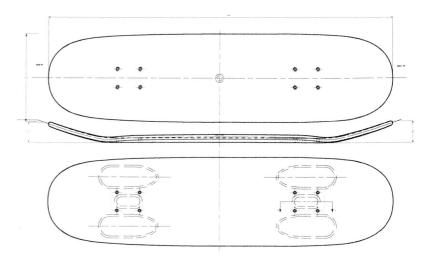

Drawings of a prototype.

FB-112 skateboard

Designers: Steen Strand (concept development and prototypes),
Matt Hern (industrial design), Dale Hinman (FB-112 engineering),
Jamie Page (FB-113 engineering), and Guthrie Dolin (graphics)
Manufacturer: Freeboard Manufacturing Inc., San Francisco,
CA, U.S.A.
Date of design: 1996–98

Snowboarding is a new sport which has become widely popular, but
conventional skateboards cannot provide the complex mix of carving
and sliding motions on the street that snowboards permit in snow.
The Freeboard has solved the problem by being configured to du-
plicate these moves. It can hug on tight turns, drift in a long, gentle
slide, flip into a "fakie," float at a "360," and permit weighting and
edging—all like a snowboard. The FB-112 makes it possible to
"snowboard" year 'round.

Wheels: Urethane.

Trucks: Aluminum A-356-T6, cold-
rolled steel, and acetal plastic.

Deck: 7-ply rock maplewood.

Production process of parts
(sourced to U.S.A. vendors):
Sand-casting, machining,
stamping, bending and molding,
cold-press wood forming, and
silkscreening (graphics).

Finishing: Grinding, belt sanding,
tumbling, and zinc plating.

Center wheels: Spring biased
for optimal control. Adjustable
height for individual riding
styles. Swivel of 360°.

Edge wheels (760mm wheel
base): "Grippy" for tight
carving.

Hangers: Very wide for stability
and control.

Trucks: Inverted kingpin for the
elimination of hangups.

Quick release: For
transformation into
a longboard.

Deck (1120mm long):
Concaved for controlled
sliding and extra wide
for controlled carving.

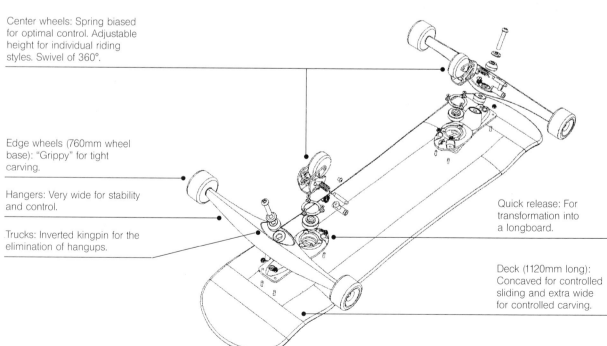

Continued on next page

FB-112 skateboard

Elements of the center wheels (right). The wheel is lifted by using your thumb to disengage the adjustment screw. Holding the adjust screw, you release the wheel. Then you lift up the wheel, and the adjustment screw automatically locks in place.

The FB-112, far more serious than it may appear, is the result of dedicated testing and numerous prototypes (examples shown below). A pre-production model was introduced in December 1997, and the final version was launched in the summer of 1998.

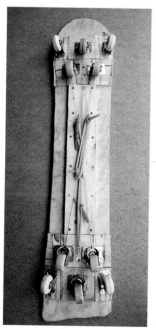

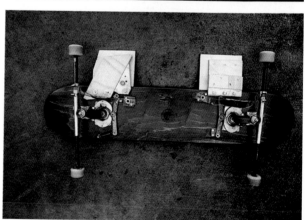

Head Gear

Hemisphere and Halfdome mountaineering helmets

Designer: Kevin Hayes, Hauser Inc.
Manufacturer: Black Diamond, Salt Lake City, UT, U.S.A.
Date of design: 1998

The assignment from the manufacturer to California designer Kevin Hayes was to create a high-performance helmet that would encourage helmet use in outdoor sports. These particular solutions—for mountaineers—are appropriate for a range of activities from rock climbing to ice climbing. Both protect the wearer from falling debris, such as rocks and ice, and provide limited protection in the event of a fall. Protection is offered against the sun and aids in keeping the head dry, with a brim to ward off rain or melting ice from the face. Integrated into the shell, a head-mounted lamp can be attached via openings that also facilitate ventilation. Simple, single adjustment is made possible by an internal suspension-and-fit system.

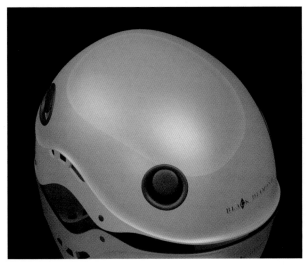

Final version of the Black Diamond model.

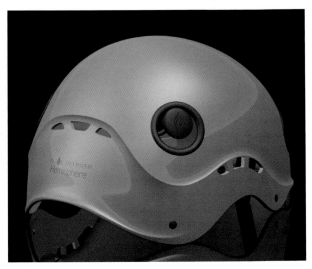

Final version of the Hemisphere model.

Study maquettes in foam.

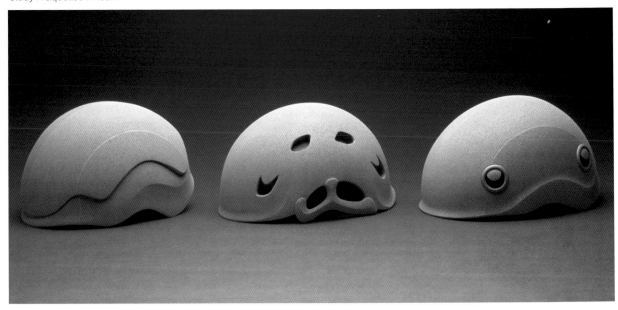

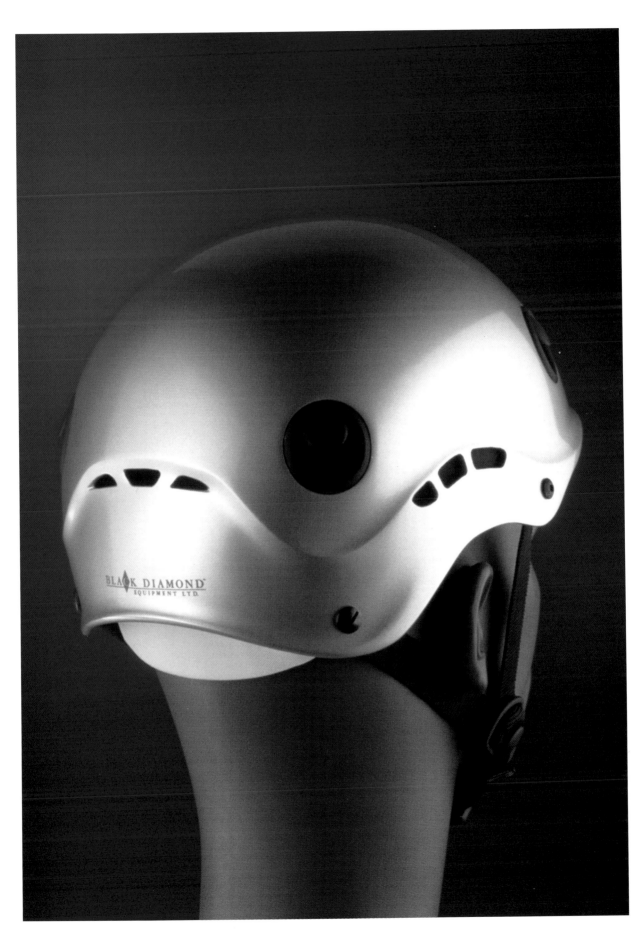

Continued on next page

Hemisphere and Halfdome mountaineering helmets

Various stages of computer-generated imaging for eventual machine tooling.

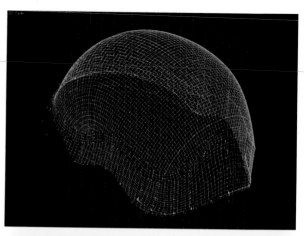

Wire-frame modeling.

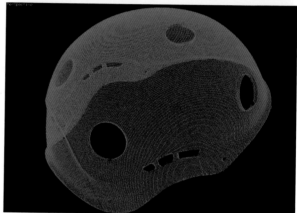

Scan-data modeling.

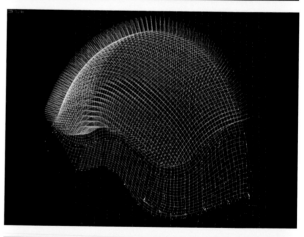

Porcupine-image modeling.

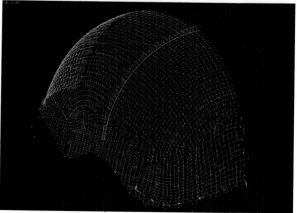

Curve-plot modeling.

The injection-molding machine houses the aluminum dies, located in the yellow cabinet (top right).

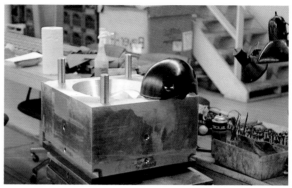

Aluminum injection-molding die.

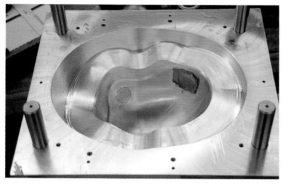

Cavity side of the die.

The rods of the cavity side fit into the holes of the core side (shown).

Soft tooling in a silicon-rubber mold.

Head-band and pit-system studies.

X-O Skeleton mountaineering helmet

Designer: Bruce M. Tharp
Manufacturer: Bruce M. Tharp, Chicago, IL, U.S.A.
Date of design: 1997

Even though a small quantity of this helmet has been produced, it has attracted a great deal of attention, especially for its unusual appearance. However, the design is an innovative one. Most helmets for cycling are used both by mountain and road bikers. The X-0 Skeleton was specifically created for the former and integrates the special technical requirements of the sport into a solution created to appeal to its potential users. According to the designer, the traditional channeling of air into bike helmets, which sends cooling currents through the helmet, are of little concern to mountain bikers who ride mostly uphill rather than down. The X-0 Skeleton provides a uniform dissipation of heat regardless of speed.

Vacuum-forming mold process.

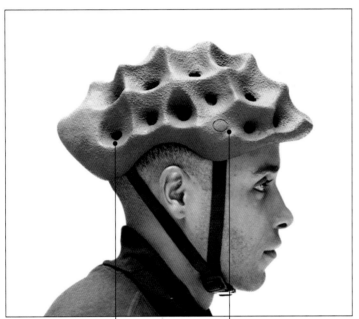

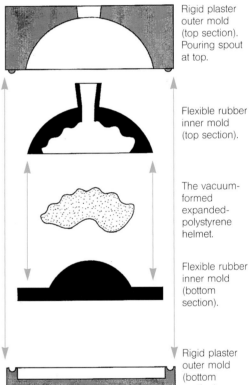

Hard-shell versions are covered with vacuum-formed polystyrene.

Air disturbance created by the protrusions increases cooling convection even at slow speeds.

The rough texture hides abrasions caused by branches, rocks, and falls.

Rigid plaster outer mold (top section). Pouring spout at top.

Flexible rubber inner mold (top section).

The vacuum-formed expanded-polystyrene helmet.

Flexible rubber inner mold (bottom section).

Rigid plaster outer mold (bottom section).

Calling on the characteristics of nature's poisonous caterpillars, cacti, alligators, sea coral, snapping turtles, certain frogs, and other animals, the helmet is available in a range of frightening-looking interpretations.

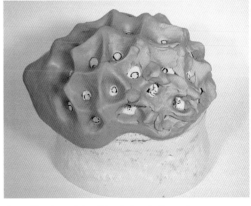

A positive template of the helmet, shown here on a holding stand, must first be made in order to build the mold.

Twinner Team bicycle-racing helmet

Designers: Fusi-Mollica-Zanotto Architetti Associati and Antonello Piredda
Manufacturer: Briko S.r.l., Dormelletto (NO), Italy
Date of design: 1997

This sleek helmet is beholden to a wide range of advanced materials
and physical technology. The streamline design appreciably decreases
wind resistance and thus helps to increase speed. Aside from equally
important factors in cycle racing—including ability, bike weight, and wind
resistance—transpiration is a major concern. The Twinner Team incorporates a system of channel intakes and outlets that create a venturi effect,
an eponym for the early 19th-century Italian physicist. A venturi is a short
tube, constricted in the middle, that causes an increase in velocity of a
flowing fluid and thus a corresponding decrease in pressure which in
turn creates suction.

Back view.

Masterized polystyrene
bearing cup.

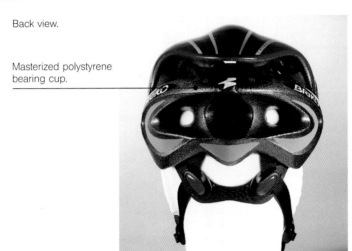

3-channel venturi effect: Suction forces hot
air through 6 slits in the inner shell.

Six air outlets allow the
escape of heat emitted
by the head.

Three front slits and
two side slits take in a
great amount of air.

The exteral cap is
fused by an in-
mold process.

Supporting shell
in GE-CET poly-
styrene and
silkscreened poly-
carbonate outer
shell are fused in
the mold.

Hytrel roll-block
system: The helmet
is adjustable by
graduated scales
for a snug fit.

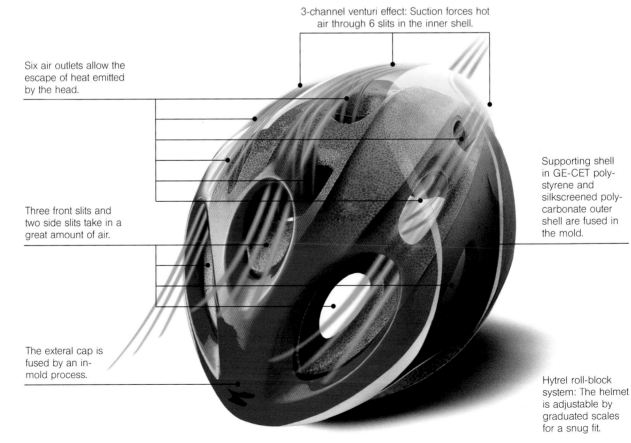

Skycap snowboard helmet

Designers: Roger Ball and Steve Copeland, Paradox Design
Manufacturer: Burton Snowboards, Burlington, VT, U.S.A.
Date of design: 1997

The first helmet to be made specifically for snowboarding has a surface that reflects the glare of powdered-snow trails, offering comfort to the wearer. The helmet was designed by Canadians for an international manufacturer known for its high-quality competition sports wares. Even though snowboarders pride themselves on being idiosyncratic, the Skycap is C.E. approved and international-specification compliant with ergonomically sound attributes. The front of the helmet offers wide peripheral vision and an open-ear design, which accommodates sun goggles and provides ventilation.

Available in three sizes.

An early-stage maquette.

A helmet shell being removed from the injection-molding die.

Continued on next page

33

Skycap snowboard helmet

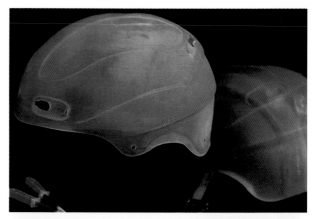

SLA (rapid prototype) (right)
determined by a CAD file.

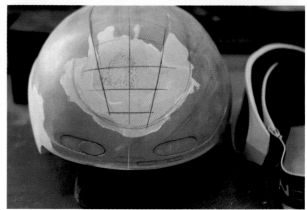

Early-stage maquettes (left and right).

Components ready for assembly.

Shell: Injection-molded polyethylene.

Liner: Compression-expanded
polypropylene beads.

Assembly: Shell taped in place.

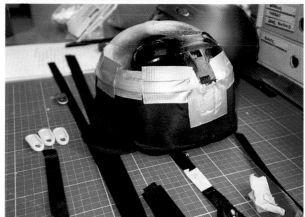

Footwear

34

TSL 217 snow shoe

Designers: Christophe Burnet and Daniel Charvat (concept), TSL Sports Equipment; Patrick Marguerit (design), Tram Design; and Fanny Mermillod (graphics), Tram Design
Manufacturer: TSL Sports Equipment—Z.A., Alex, France
Date of design: 1998

A highly successful product, the manufacturer produces 40,000 pairs of this snow shoe a year. The configuration assures optimal security in all snow conditions and terrain, works well on difficult passages, has a long life, and resists low temperatures and extreme conditions. Its offbeat appearance probably appeals to young winter-sports enthusiasts.

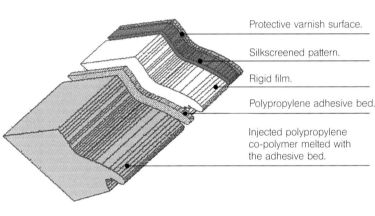

Protective varnish surface.

Silkscreened pattern.

Rigid film.

Polypropylene adhesive bed.

Injected polypropylene co-polymer melted with the adhesive bed.

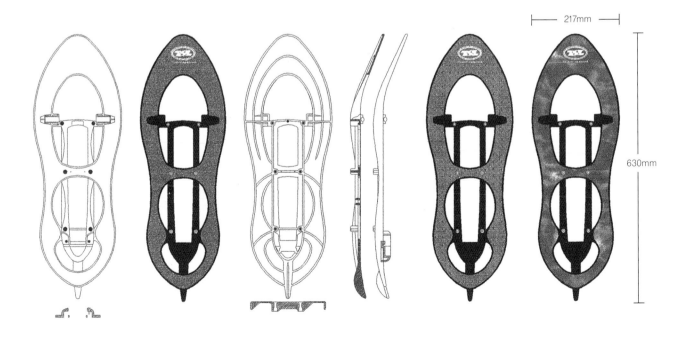

217mm

630mm

35

Action crampon

Designers: Cassin research-&-development staff
Manufacturer: Cassin S.r.l., Valitadrera (LC), Italy
Date of design: 1998

Located in the Italian Alps, in 1909 the Grivel family invented and began making the world's first modern crampons from the best-quality steel available at the time. Old railroad ties were cut up, reheated, and forged by hand. Better-quality steel is available today, like that used by another Italian forger, Cassin. When used for crampons, the new harder steel offers deeper ice penetration and lessens the need for sharpening. However, the design and function of the crampons themselves have essentially changed little over the years, with the exception of Laurent Grivel's 12-point version, created in 1932.

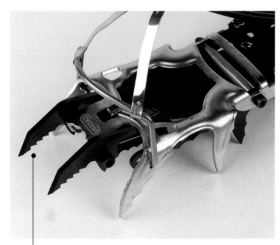

Forging of Ni-Cro-Mo (chromoly) steel, similar to stainless steel, begins with a 3mm-thick strap-iron section in an annealed state. It is heated and cooled and becomes soft enough to shape. After shaping, the piece is oven heated for tempering. The heat treatment enhances the properties of the steel. Slag is sandblasted away, and the piece is electronically powder-coated with an epoxy-based paint. Finally, the crampon is oven cured to polymerize the paint for a uniform thickness.

Removable rear tooth (supplied separately) for heel anchorage in extreme positions.

Flexible front bail (a covered metal cable) for a snug fit on all types of boots.

Teeth on all points.

Vertical element of rear section offers high resistance and eliminates vibration.

Safety binding system permits quick release.

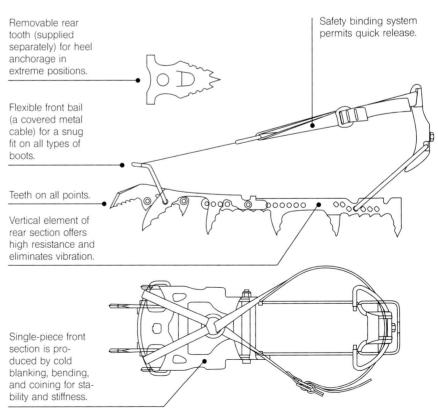

Single-piece front section is produced by cold blanking, bending, and coining for stability and stiffness.

36

Pinna V-Drive swim fin

Designers: Oceanic Europe technical staff with Bonetto Design
Manufacturer: Oceanic Europe S.r.l., Rome, Italy
Date of design: 1994

A design studio collaborated with a manufacturer's technical staff, a standard practice in the sports-equipment industry today, to create the Pinna V-Drive swim fin. The manufacturer's goal was to make the most technically efficient fin possible. Human physiology, including the behavior of the group of muscles used in the kicking cycle, was analyzed. The muscles at the back of the leg, comprising the hamstring and those of the calf, are the weakest primary muscles of the leg. The muscles on the front of the leg are used in the down or power stroke; those at the back are used in the up or recovery stroke. The design of the Pinna V-Drive fin was based on these basic biomechanical principles.

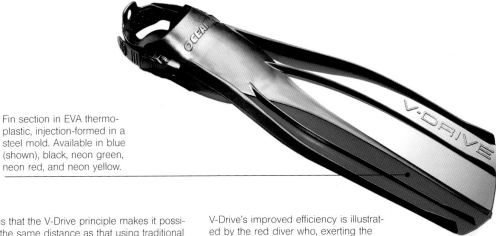

Fin section in EVA thermo-plastic, injection-formed in a steel mold. Available in blue (shown), black, neon green, neon red, and neon yellow.

The manufacturer claims that the V-Drive principle makes it possible for a diver to cover the same distance as that using traditional fin blades with noticeably less applied force or energy.

V-Drive's improved efficiency is illustrated by the red diver who, exerting the same amount of effort, travels farther.

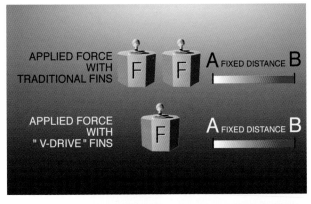

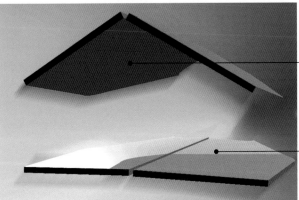

The computer-generated image demonstrates variable surface ratio and variable power. In the recovery stroke, maximum efficiency with the least effort is possible when the lateral surface area is smaller.

Variable power—proportional to the force exerted on the blade—is produced during the power stroke when the lateral surface area is larger.

The dynamics of the Prinna V-Drive are effective no matter an individual swimmer's leg strength, physical size, or athletic ability.

Regular Force, Extra Force, and Excellerating Force Fins with Whiskers

Designer: Bob Evans
Manufacturer: Bob Evans Design Inc., Santa Barbara, CA, U.S.A.
Date of design: 1981 and 1995

Obsessed from an early age with the ocean and its wonders, Bob Evans is an accomplished diver and underwater photographer as well as a pioneering inventor of scuba-diving equipment. His design of efficient swim fins was inspired by the mobility of sea creatures, like the squid, tuna, and porpoise. He studied the fins of fast-swimming fish and experimented with numerous swim-fin configurations before producing a prototype made of chicken wire covered with newspaper and a resin. After 15 years of research and in-water use, Evans arrived at the Force Fin principle.

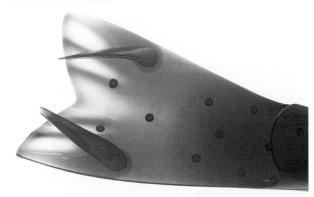

Extra Force Fin model.

Excellerating Force Fin model.

Flexible blades facilitate a 2-stroke kick cycle, create better water channeling, and diminish recovery resistance.

Strap of parachute webbing with a swivel buckle and heel pad.

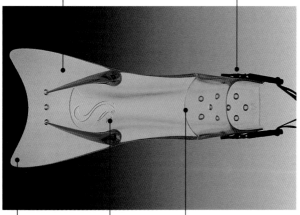

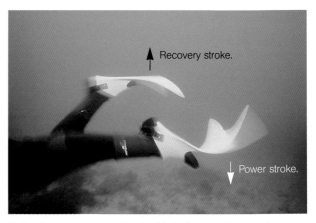

Recovery stroke.

Power stroke.

Flexible blade tip moves independently for better control and movement.

Internal ribs steady the blade action.

Open-toe design reduces toe and foot cramping.

In the down or power stroke, the blade flays out for a maximum surface area, requiring the work of the leg's front, or most powerful, muscles. In the up or recovery stroke, the blade returns to its original, or memory-retaining, state, thrusting the swimmer forward.

Continued on next page

Regular Force, Extra Force, and Excellerating Force Fins

Prototypes (right and below).

Bob Evans at work on a mold. Fins are cast in polyurethane, hand trimmed, pour-spew cut, spew-scar ground cleaned, band sawn and sanded, and drilled.

Shop manufacture (left and below).

A workman sand finishes a
fin. Straps are attached with
stainless-steel screws.

Inventory.

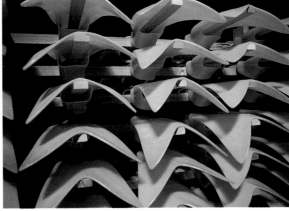

38

Wave Lazer running shoe

Designers: Mizuno Research-&-Development Department
Manufacturer: Mizuno Corporation, Osaka, Japan
Date of design: 1998

It is difficult to stand out in the sea of sports and running shoes available today, and manufacturers are indefatigable in their pursuit to stay ahead of the fray. Mizuno, one of the leaders in the field, has developed what it calls Wave technology, based on biomechanical principles. Its research and development team conducted extensive laboratory tests on numerous materials, including polyurethane and Pebax. Founded on studies of the foot and the human body and how they work during various athletic activities, the results of Mizuno's efforts have been realized in almost thirty shoe types in a range appropriate for specific competition sports, such as football, shot-put, jumping, and javelin throwing. The Wave Lazer model shown here is for running.

Intended for rapid running, the Lazer Wave model features a semi-curved sole, weighs 300g and is available in grey, black, yellow, blue, or red.

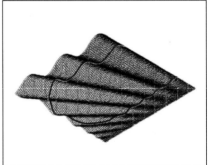

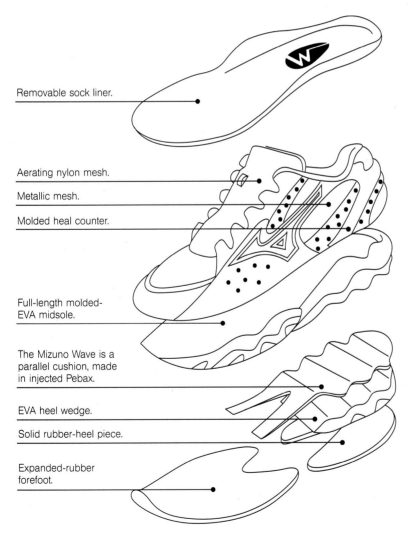

Removable sock liner.

Aerating nylon mesh.

Metallic mesh.

Molded heal counter.

Full-length molded-EVA midsole.

The Mizuno Wave is a parallel cushion, made in injected Pebax.

EVA heel wedge.

Solid rubber-heel piece.

Expanded-rubber forefoot.

Based on biomechanical principles, including the knowledge that the impact on a sports shoe is 3 to 5 times a person's weight, the Mizuno research staff developed the Wave sole and its effective employment in various shoe models to be suitable for numerous competitive sports.

39

Reactor snowboard boot

Designers: MM Design S.r.l.
Manufacturer: Burton Snowboards, Innsbruck, Austria
Date of design: 1993

The snowboard, which originated in America, has become popular on European ski slopes. But, due to the conditions of this terrain, Europeans are demanding a more rigid boot than that being used by Americans. Burton, the distinguished American sports-equipment manufacturer, chose an Italian design studio to create a boot specific to Continental snowboarding that was missing in the marketplace. Calling on the expertise of the Burton staff, the designers studied the technical and functional requirements as they pertained to materials and mechanical performance to arrive at a product that would appeal to a young customer.

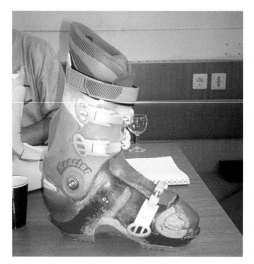

Early-stage prototype.

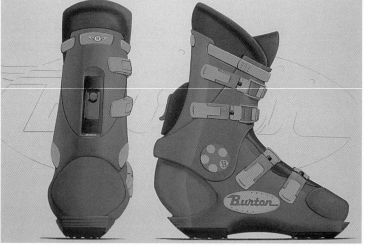

The highly inclined heel and toe, shown in this rendering, is more adaptable to the new generation of narrower boards.

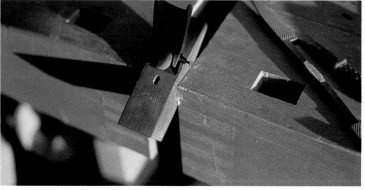

This painted maquette illustrates the elastic form that binds the foot and offers a feeling of lightness and practicality. The design is sculpted to the foot to permit the easy movement of a boarder's forefoot, heel, and tibia, making it possible to transmit this movement accurately to the board. The comfortable innersole includes leather at the top where it contacts the leg directly.

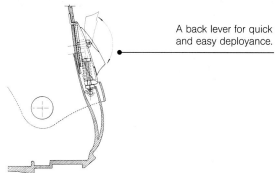

A back lever for quick and easy deployance.

Carv X ski boot

Designers: Design Continuum Italia
Manufacturer: Atomic Sport GmbH, Altenmarkt, Austria
Date of design: 1996–97

Carving is a highly demanding technique when an Alpine skier is being hurled down a slope at a high speed. Great demands are made on equipment, including boots appropriate for carving. Both the boot innard and the shell must be specifically configured to the sport itself for the best support and flexibility. Design Continuum Italia conducted tests on ski-slopes before the staff began the actual design process in the studio. The solution satisfies the demands of the most highly proficient skiers. A double-molding process eliminates the necessity of glue and rivets in order to facilitate disassembly and subsequent recycling of individual parts.

Overall boot size 310mm long, 130mm wide, 350mm high; weight 3.05kg.

Injection-molded polyurethane.

Double injection-molding combines a structurally rigid lower part with a softer, more supple upper part that is tightly sealed.

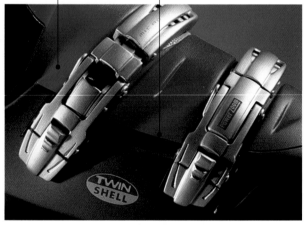

The shell in two parts provides rigidity at the back and sides, thus offering a great deal of support in critical areas.

The supple front end fits tightly but is flexible.

Nickel-plated aluminum "power zoom" buckles with titanium straps provide micro-adjustmentability and hold the foot comfortably and securely.

A polycarbonate support set into the sole prevents dangerous twisting.

Continued on next page

Carv X ski boot

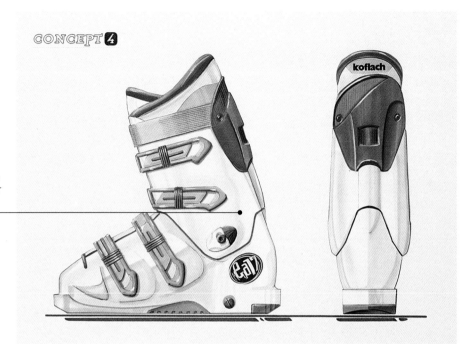

The concept drawing (right) reveals the system that allows lateral canting of both the shell and the inner boot; this is due to what the designers describe as the "edge-sensitive system." The optimized angle provides friction-minimized power transmission for instantaneous direction changes.

Believing color to be of great importance, the designers conducted color studies (below) before specifying the precise color, according to the PMS color system, of every part and piece.

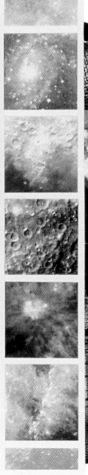

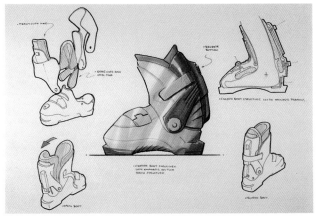

Concept studies concerning
color, function, shape, construction, and segmentation.

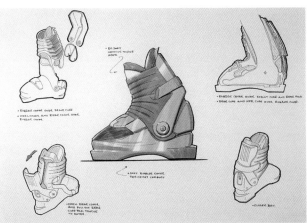

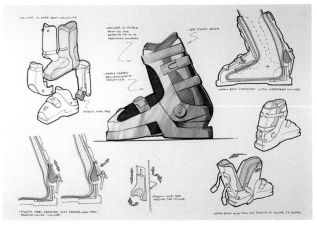

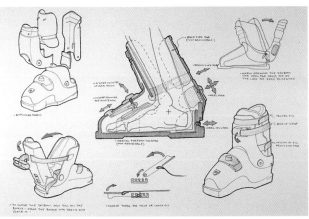

Y-Tech 100 Degree mountaineering boot

Designers: Design Continuum Italia
Manufacturer: Koflach Sport GmbH, Köflach, Austria, for Atomic Sport
Date of design: 1996–97

This mountaineering boot is part of a system of footwear which includes boot shells, various liners, five different matching socks, and gaiters. The boot, featuring highly functional lacing and hardware, makes trekking in different Alpine situations comfortable. Available in a range of other models, the 100 Degree version shown here was designed to contend with the most rigorous climactic conditions found in high altitudes. A choice of removable liners varies according to individual requirements. The most distinctive feature of the Y-Tech line, which received the 1998 iF Product Design Award, may be its light weight.

The push-and-grip-zoned natural-rubber sole by Vibrate is self-cleaning.

Responsive shock-dampening heel lessens walking and hiking fatigue.

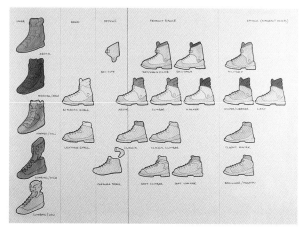

A conceptual drawing illustrates boot types and construction.

The lacing system permits safe and easy fastening.

The lower 3 pairs of lace holders are a patented steel-ball mechanism. The laces slide smoothly and ensure consistent pressure, even in low temperatures.

The shell and tongue are waterproof.

The soft thermoplastic forefoot is co-injected with the polyurethane shell of the hard midsection and upper cuff.

The rigid, durable midsole provides for the reliable application of crampons and kit bindings.

Continued on next page

Y-Tech mountaineering boot

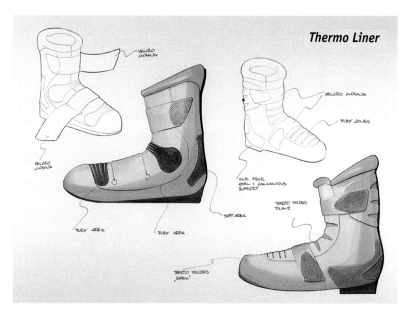

Thermo Liner

The designers' conceptual drawings illustrate the thermal liner
(right) and components of the
midsole and metal fittings, including the rigid Twist'a Bar insert
(below).

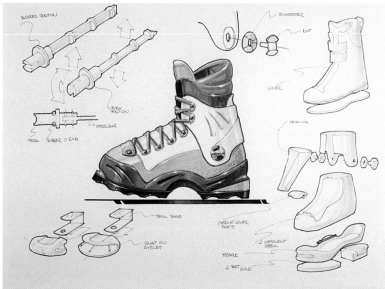

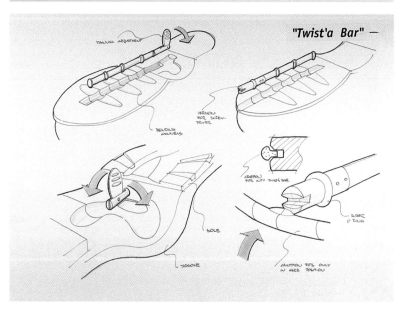

"Twist'a Bar" —

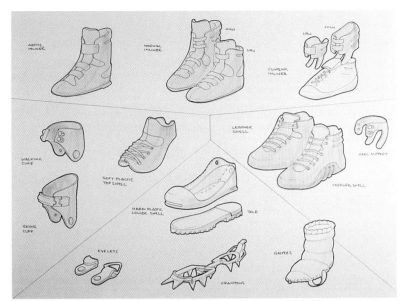

Various conceptual models and fittings illustrate walking and skiing cuffs, the sole design, lacing eyelets, and the climbing inliner.

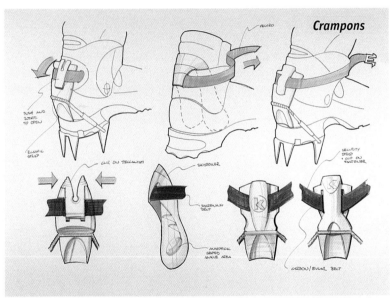

Crampon attachment.

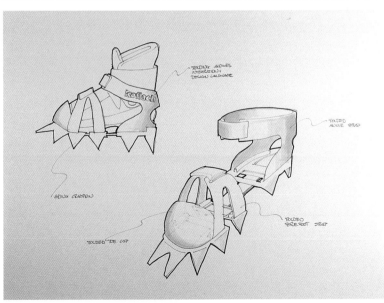

t'blade ice-hockey skates

Designers: Dan Harden and staff, frog inc.
Manufacturer: Würthner Sport Technologie, VS-Schwenningen, Germany
Date of design: 1997

The new skating blade of this revolutionary design melts the ice
beneath and, thus, increases skater speed. The very thin replaceable
blade is co-molded into a plastic substrate before being clamped onto
the glass-impregnated nylon base of the boot. The manufacturer claims
the blade to be 0.04mm thick; the designers purport 0.7mm thick which,
at either measure, is very thin. Professional ice-hockey players, who
notoriously treat equipment brutally, rely on skates that will withstand
abrupt, brisk movements and harsh treatment. Since grinding to sharp-
en skate blades promotes drag and increases rough edges, a skater's
speed is slowed down. The manufacturer turned to the frog design
staff for an alternative to the traditional sharpening of conventional
hardened-steel blades and for a completely new solution to ice-hockey
skate design.

The lightweight but very
rigid glass-impregnated
blade bracket was made
possible by the use of
advanced materials and
CAD-modeling tech-
niques. The full unit
weighs 160g compared
to the 300g typical of
traditional skates.

A 0.7mm-thick strip of
steel—replaceable like
a razor blade—is co-
molded into a plastic
substrate. Since the metal
is very thin, the blade
heats up and melts the
rink ice beneath to pro-
duce a 25% faster speed.

Continued on next page

t'blade ice hockey skate

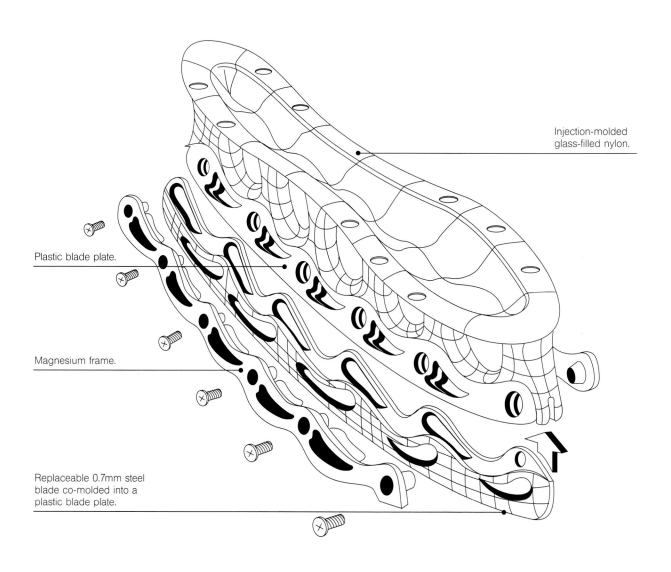

Injection-molded glass-filled nylon.

Plastic blade plate.

Magnesium frame.

Replaceable 0.7mm steel blade co-molded into a plastic blade plate.

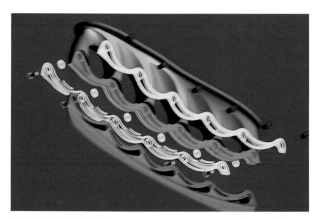

Exploded ProE CAD drawing of the blade and blade plates.

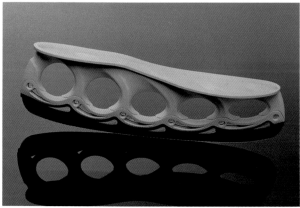

Assembled and disassembled models.

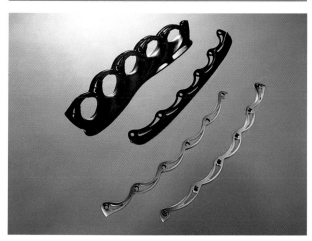

43

Clapskate

Designers: Franz Krienbühl (boot and blade) and Peter van der Klok
(Clap mechanism)
Manufacturer: Alfred Tanner, Biel, Switzerland (boot and blade), and
Finn B.V., Groningen, The Netherlands (Clap mechanism)
Date: 1998

Purported to be the lightest skate found anywhere, the boot, understructure, and blade components contribute to a marked weight reduction. The unique feature of the skate is the hinged blade. The base of the boot hinges open when the skater's foot is lifted after each push, making it possible for the blade to stay on the ice surface longer than with traditional skates. On the subsequent pushes, the back end of the blade glides onto the ice, rather than, as with traditional skates, digging into the ice on the front end and thus slowing a skater's speed. The skate comes equipped with a blade-sharpening tool, and the boot base can be adapted to inline-skate use.

Primarily intended for speed-skating use, the boot base will accommodate an inline-skate frame.

Orthopedic foot-bed shell.

The light skating boot, weighing less than most other boots, in kangaroo leather. Soft inner lining. Achilles-tendon band for injury prevention.

Blade, interchangeable for different ice conditions, in stainless steel, produced through a special chemical process to provide excellent glide under various weather conditions.

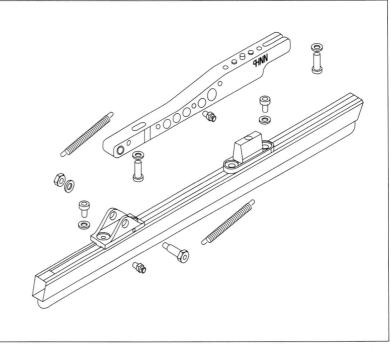

The 16 different components of the skating blade are revealed by an exploded drawing.

Metroblade inline skate

Designers: Design Continuum, Inc., Boston office
Manufacturer: Rollerblade, Inc., Minnetonka, MN, U.S.A.
Date of design: 1992

Rollerblade was not the inventor of inline skates but pioneered the boom by changing public perception. In 1980, a pair of inline skates was discovered by two Minnesota hockey-playing brothers who decided to refit them. This advent resulted in the adoption of the skate by professional hockey players and soon Nordic and Alpine skiers for off-season training. In 1983, when the company was sold, aggressive marketing began. Rollerbade, whose name is now used generically much to the dismay of the firm, has introduced a number of innovations including polyurethane boots and wheels, metal frames, dual bearings, heel brakes, and, subsequently, lightweight non-metal frames. The ever-changing nature of sports technology is evident in a comparison of the 1992 Rollerblade here with a 1997 design (pages 134–136) by the Italian office of Continuum for Oxygen Sport.

The shoe is easily removable from the shell with one buckle (facing page). Its padded construction is made of Lycra, neoprene, leather, and cordura. The semi-rigid polyurethane tongue acts as a scuff plate between the shoe and the cuff of the shell.

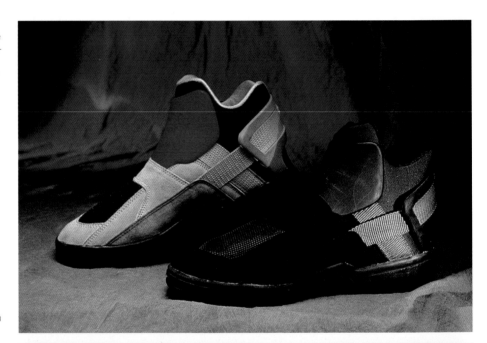

The colors were chosen to appeal to young adults and students. The liner can be used as a shoe separate from the shell/bracket unit.

Polyurethane cuff.

To decrease manufacturing costs, the one-piece lower shell and blade bracket is co-molded of nylon with glass-reinforcement in the blade bracket. Nylon offers strength and support.

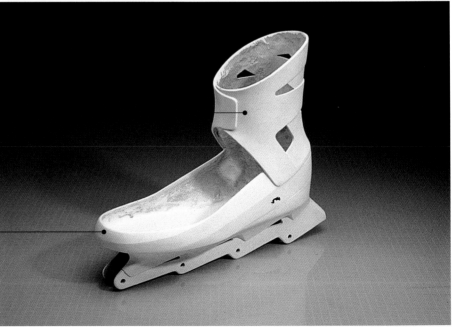

Continued on next page

44

Metroblade inline skate

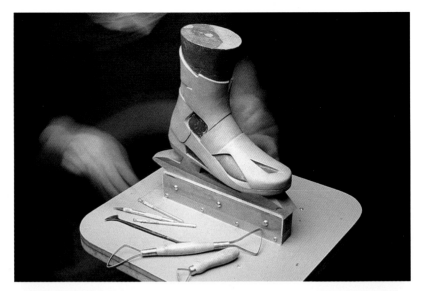

Early-stage maquettes.

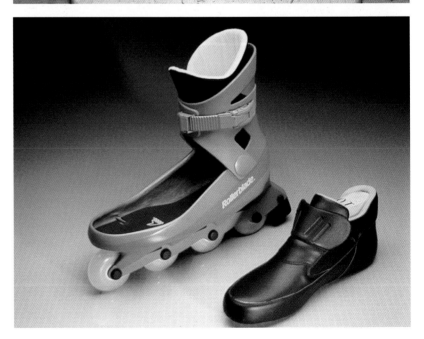

Shell, liner, and removable shoe.

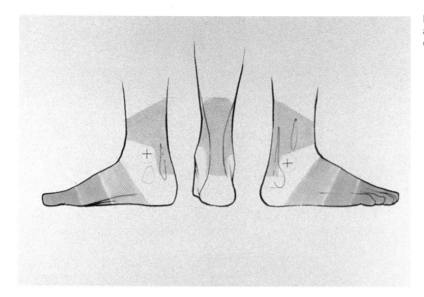

Foot studies of the clamping areas considered best for optimal comfort and support.

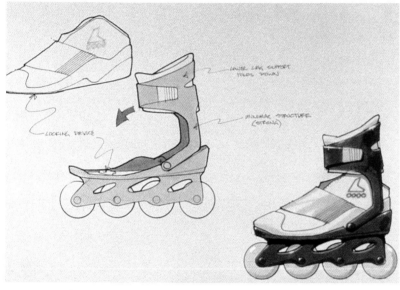

A preliminary drawing focuses on the flexible cuff and illustrates the inner-shoe insertion.

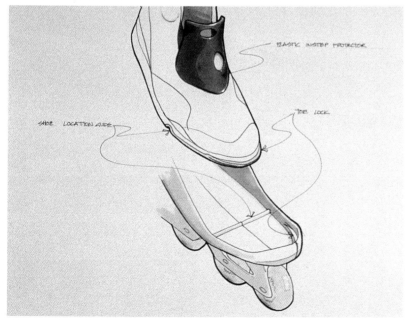

A conceptual drawing of the plastic instep protector and shoe insertion.

Oz-One inline skate

Designers: Design Continuum Italia
Manufacturer: Oxygen Sport GmbH, Köflach, Austria
Date of design: 1996–97

The Oz-One inline skate was the first to incorporate the rigidity of a plastic shell with the comfort of a sports shoe. The exceptionally lightweight skate was designed to appeal to young urban customers, male and female. For breathability, plastic was specified only in areas where support and fastening are required. High-end wheels and easy-to-deploy buckles are included in the reasonably priced Oz-One. Compare the skates with the 1992 version (pages 130–133) for Rollerblade design by the Boston office of Design Continuum.

With the attributes of a ski boot, the 4 colors of the skate include a version for women, for whom a specially adapted shell was developed.

Ergonomically positioned hinge point between the cuff and shell.

Maximum breathability of the inner boot was realized through a new type of sandwich structure in perforated polyethylene and nylon mesh. The materials are fused by a dry-joining process.

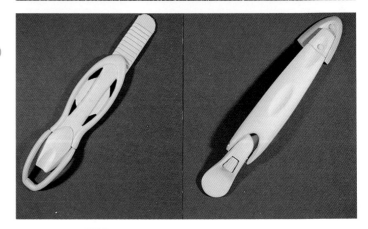

The placement of buckles (prototypes at right) and the hinge around which the cuff turns on the shell (above right) were a result of extensive studies of the relationship of the foot and the skate.

Four high-quality 76mm wheels are standard components.

Continued on next page

Oz-One inline skate

Conceptual drawings of the
sliding rotational point where
the foot naturally flexes.

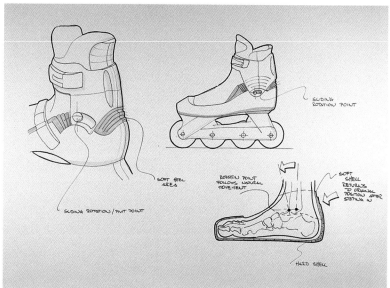

An example of the kind of
in-depth studies of the foot
conducted by the design team.

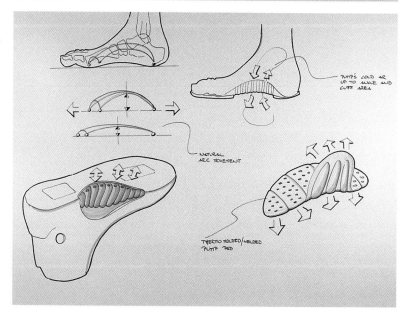

Etcetera

Scan 'O' Vision Pro photo-finish machine

Designers: Swiss Timing staff
Manufacturer: Omega—Swiss Timing Ltd., a company of SMH, Saint-Imier, Switzerland
Date of design: 1966 and ongoing developments

The photo finish, a combination of a time detector and a chronograph, was developed by amalgamating chronometry and chronophotography (the capture and analysis of movement in time). The first instantaneous photos of racing finishes occurred in America in 1886 and was first used at the Olympics in 1912 at Stockholm. But, in 1942, M.I.T. physicist Arthur C. Hardy determined that continuous-recording devices were superior to frame-by-frame systems. Developed in 1945, Omega, a specialist in photo-finish recording that uses continuous film, introduced the principle for the first time at the Olympics in 1948 in London. The Scan 'O' Vision system, shown here, became the first continuous-image electronic recording device to combine precision and practicality.

The continuous-image recording device records continuous images at different speeds and transfers them without distortion onto a single-speed video recorder. Two recordings are produced: one on magnetic tape and the other as stored static-image memory. The chronograph and time detector are linked.

An image (left) of the finish line of the final men's 100m dash at the 1996 Summer Olympic Games in Atlanta.

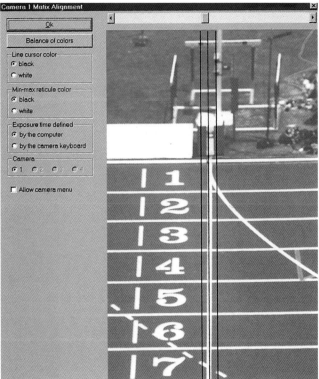

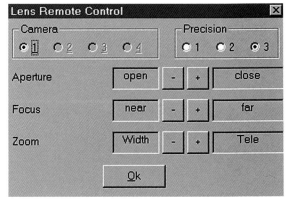

Photo-finish technology has been converted to personal-computer technology. The remote-control software (monitor window above) can adjust the zoom, focus, and aperture controls of the lens.

Fine adjustment of the video alignment is electronically possible. The software permits the repositioning of the lines (shown by the black vertical lines at left) used for timing within a range of 16 increments.

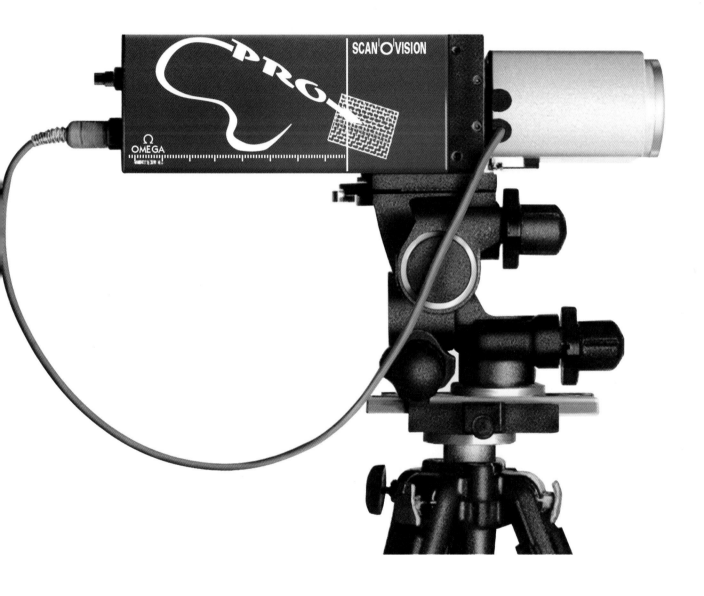

Continued on next page

Scan 'O' Vision Pro photo-finish machine

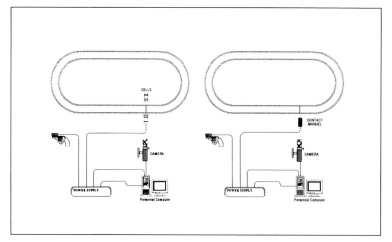

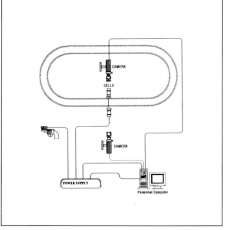

The diagram above illustrates the normal set-up of the Scan 'O' Vision system. The camera (red boxes) is outside the track (ovoid lines). The camera, the light barrier for the time-taking and for the automatic starting of the video recording, and the starter pistol are all connected to a power supply and a personal computer.

A 2-camera set-up, outside the track on each side of the finish line, can recognize a competitor who may be hidden.

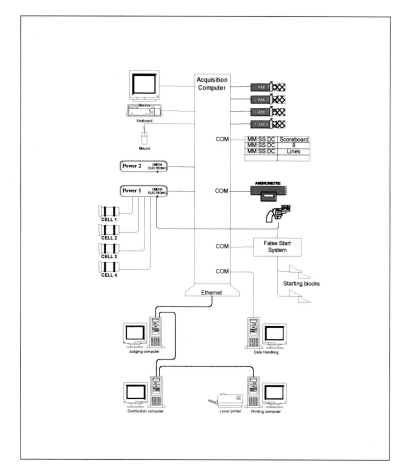

This diagram shows the maximum configuration of the system—4 cameras and 4 photocells. The camera and the cells can be placed in different locations along a race course to allow for interim time-takes. A common configuration includes two opposite cameras that will record participants from each side of the finish line. In most cases, 4 cameras and 2 recording personal computers are used for full redundancy.

At Stockholm in 1912, the Omega photo-finish system was first used at an Olympic event. Official time-takers at the 1500m race included a photographer at the top of the stairs. The image of the finish helped to determine the 2nd-place runner (Kiviat of the U.S.A.) from the 3rd-place runner (Traber of the U.S.A.).

Regularly used from 1935–45, 4 Omega chronographs in a box were connected to a starter pistol. The chronographs were the same as those used at the 1932 Olympic Games in Los Angeles.

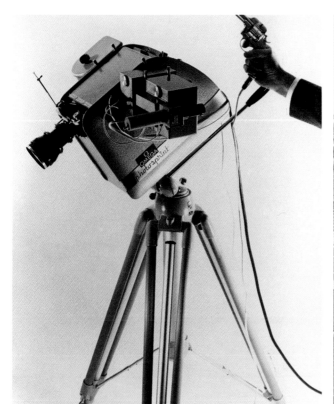

The Omega Photosprint, developed in 1963, filmed all athletes at the finish line. Time differences within 1/100 increments were shown as spatial differences in a photograph available within 30 seconds after the race. The results become the determinant in very close races.

The track-and-field European championship games in 1966 at Budapest were the first time the current Omega Photosprint was officially used in competition. 24 officials (3 for each track) used stopwatches as a backup.

47

Speedo Stroke monitors

Designer: Fred Bould
Manufacturer: Stroke Digital Sports, Inc., Dallas, TX, U.S.A.,
for Speedo
Date of design: 1997

Speedo Stroke monitors are state-of-the-art training tools
that register instantaneous quantitative feedback for swim-
ming performance. While there are two different monitors
for professionals and for sports enthusiasts, they look alike.
These monitors are the only swimming-training devices
that automatically count strokes and provide meaningful
quantitative feedback. The monitors were designed to
resemble wristwatches.

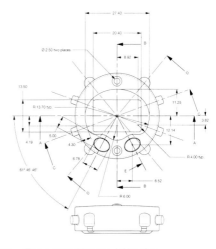

The competitive model tracks:
Stroke cycle
Elapsed time
Distance per stroke cycle
Stroke cycle per minute
Speed in yards or meters per second
SEI (Swim Efficiency Index) =
(distance/time in seconds +
number of stroke cycles) x 100

The fitness model tracks:
Calories burned
Distance swum
Stroke cycle per minute
Elapsed time

Injection-molded ABS case.

Clear acrylic lens, ultrasoni-
cally welded to the case.

ASICs embedded in the
back-lit LCD watch module.

Injection-molded polyure-
thane strap, identical
on both models.

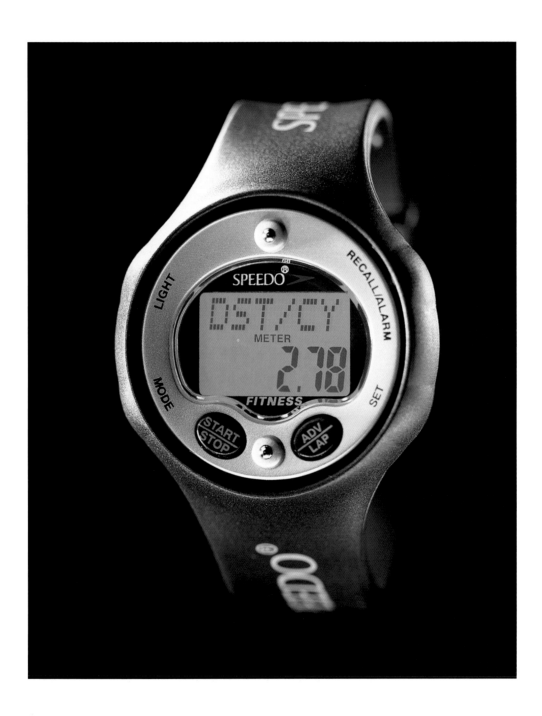

Continued on next page

48

Smart Home Fitness

Designers: Xavier Moulin and Aldo Cibic
Manufacturer: Xavier Moulin, Paris
Date of design: 1998

A response to the recent cult of sports and the desire for in-home exercise equipment, Smart Home Fitness was created as an alternative to what the designers call "encumbering fitness machinery." The setting became a traveling exhibition which premiered at the Internos gallery during the 1998 furniture fair in Milan. The designers suggested that people might use their home in the way skaters use the city—to playful and sporting ends. The Smart Home Fitness system is presumed to stimulate the mind, body, and interpersonal relationships in a free, imaginative manner—not through body-building equipment but pieces of furniture that double as exercise equipment. The ten configurations are represented here by Moulin's drawings.

Up/down.

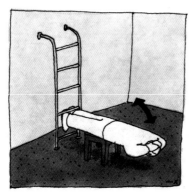

Throne.

Ladder.

Chaise longue.

Free ride

Frog walk.

Free climb.

Corner.

Sand.

Pause.

49

Institutional furniture for the Olympiad

Designer: Martin Székely
Manufacturer: Satragno, France, (referee and players seats) and
C.N.D.B. (Comité national pour le développement du bois), France,
(winners' podium).
Date of design: 1992–93 and subsequently

The commissioning of Martin Székely to design the institutional furniture for the 1992 Winter Olympics held in Albertville, France, and
1993 French Open tennis tournament is testament to the thorough
approach the French committees took to organizing the events. The
winners' podium broke from the anonymous, plain boxes normally
found at sports events. After the games, examples of the podium
were acquired by F.N.A.C. (Fonds national d'art contemporain) in
France and the Musée du sport in Switzerland.

The tennis referee's chair (2,200mm high, 1,050mm diameter) is
wood and metal, painted light and dark green.

The sideline seats of the athletes (1,840mm long, 600mm wide,
1,000mm high) are also wood and metal, painted light and dark
green with applied sponsor logos.

The winners' podium (3,490mm long, 830mm wide, 1,860mm
high) was constructed of pinewood and metal, painted yellow.

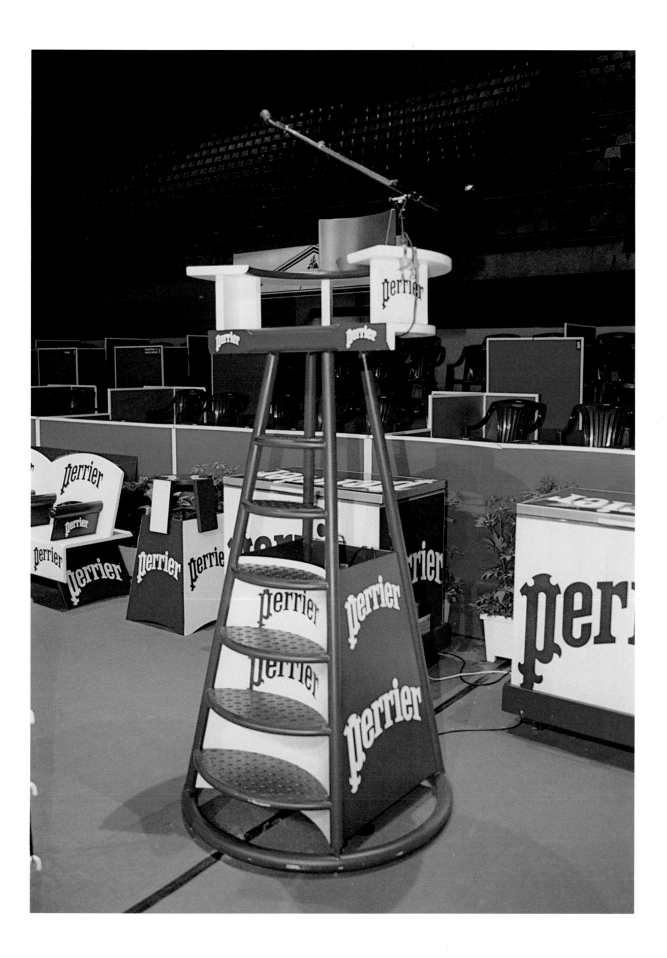

AstroTurf play surfaces

Designers: Chemstrand Corporation
Manufacturer: Southwest Recreational Industries, Leander, TX, U.S.A.
Date of design: 1964 and subsequently

AstroTurf was originally developed with a Ford Foundation grant in the early 1960s. Studies of Korean War inductees indicated that the most physically fit soldiers were those who had grown up in rural areas with wide-open space for play. This led to the decision to create an all-weather, grass-like playing surface applicable in tight city spaces. The Chemstrand Corporation developed the product in 1964 that was first offered to the small Morris Brown School in Providence, Rhode Island. When the Astrodome was built in 1966 in Houston, TX, grass could not be grown indoors. The product, originally called ChemTurf, was renamed AstroTurf after the breakthrough installation. Today there are AstroTurf fields in over forty countries. Several versions of AstroTurf for different sports are available, including AstroPlay shown here.

The texturized Nylon 66 fiber resists matting and crushing. It offers a positive performance which does not change and facilitates uniform traction and ball roll.

Hydrophilic nylon fibers absorb water. AstroGrass, combined with sand movement, has the characteristics of wet pitch.

The pen-cell foam pad acts as a cushion and retains water, creating a "pump and play" feature.

Sand dressing, not sand filling. The play is on the green, grass-like surface, not on the sand.

The system may be placed over an asphalt, concrete, elastic, or other suitable surface.

Porous system for vertical water drainage.

Generally the AstroTurf product is a nylon fiber knitted to a polyester backing. The fabric is adhered to one of a variety of shock pads—normally a closed-cell elastomeric foam. The pile fiber is highly texturized and fixed by the use of light. Manufacturing machinery includes custom-engineered extrusion devices, drawing and texturing equipment, and special knitting looms. Assembly (example at right) is on-site, adhered to a substrate with a moisture-curing monocomponent-polyurethane adhesive spray. The seams of 15ft-wide sections are sewn together.

Continued on next page

AstroTurf

A quench bath cools the fibers for drawing and texturing.

The backing fibers are drawn from rollers.

From ribbon spindles, nylon is mixed with a knitted backing.

A weaving machine knits fibers into a single fabric.

Designers and Design Staffs
Manufacturers
Credits

Designers and Design Staffs

Manufacturers

Photography and Art Credits

General Index

General Index